healthy meals for healthy kids

healthy meals for healthy kids

80 DELICIOUS RECIPES FOR KIDS OF ALL AGES

CATHERINE ATKINSON

NEW HOLLAND

First published in 2008 by New Holland Publishers (UK) Ltd
London • Cape Town • Sydney • Auckland

Garfield House
86–88 Edgware Road
London W2 2EA
United Kingdom
www.newhollandpublishers.com

80 McKenzie Street
Cape Town 8001
South Africa

Unit 1, 66 Gibbes Street
Chatwood
NSW 2067
Australia

218 Lake Road
Northcote
Auckland
New Zealand

ISBN 978 1 84537 991 9

Senior Editor: Corinne Masciocchi
Designer: Lucy Parissi
Photographer: Ian Garlick
Home economy and food styling: Nikki Gee
Production: Hema Gohil
Editorial Direction: Rosemary Wilkinson

2 4 6 8 10 9 7 5 3 1

Reproduction by Pica Digital PTE Ltd, Singapore
Printed and bound by Tien Wah Press, Singapore

contents

introduction

A well-balanced diet will give your child the best possible start in life. Those who eat a healthy, varied diet are more likely to be full of energy, suffer fewer illnesses and be more attentive at school. Children grow rapidly between the ages of five and 12, gaining an average of 5–7.5 cm (2–3 in) in height each year. To support this rapid growth and development, they need a good supply of nutrients, especially protein, calcium and iron. It's not just a child's body that needs good nourishment, though. Many nutrients, especially the B vitamins and iron, are important for concentration and learning, and the brain needs a constant supply of glucose and oxygen. Teenagers have higher nutritional needs than any other group, yet often have the poorest diet, choosing the easy option of processed and fast foods. Encouraging good food habits from an early age could have a significant effect on health throughout adolescence and in later life, and could help protect against problems such as osteoporosis, heart disease and some cancers.

The recipes in this book are about striking a balance between healthy eating and food that children enjoy. Eating well shouldn't mean boring meals or denying favourite foods, but rather providing a diet that is healthy and varied, as well as delicious.

So much has been written in the past decade about what children shouldn't eat that most of us are well aware that too many sugary, fatty, or over-processed foods should be avoided. But healthy eating is not about deprivation; the secret lies in serving more foods that will promote wellbeing and that children enjoy.

Eat more protein-rich foods

As well as growth and the repair of muscles, skin and other tissues, protein is needed to make antibodies and hormones. Because children grow rapidly, they need more protein and calories proportionally for their body weight than adults. Protein is found in meat and fish, dairy produce such as cheese and milk, and many plant sources, including pulses, grains and nuts. During digestion, protein is broken down into building blocks known as amino acids. There are 25 different ones, but only eight are 'essential', i.e. they must be provided by the diet. If your child doesn't eat meat or fish, plant proteins can be combined so that missing amino acids from one type can be provided by those in another. For instance, most cereals lack an amino acid called lysine, and pulses do not contain methionine, but if you serve a bean casserole with rice, all necessary amino acids will be provided. Children between the ages of five and six need around 20 g of protein daily; this rises to around 28 g between the ages of seven and 10; and 42 g for 11- and 12-year-olds.

Food	Protein per serving (g)
75 g (2½ oz) roast chicken, beef, lamb or pork	20
100 g (3½ oz) white fish	18
Two fish fingers	7
Two vegetarian (Quorn) sausages	12
25 g (¼ cup) peanuts	6
225 ml (1 cup) glass of milk	8
150 g (⅔ cup) plain or fruit yoghurt	8
Matchbox-size piece of Cheddar cheese	12

Eat more starchy carbohydrates

The brain and body cells rely entirely on broken-down carbohydrates (glucose) to function, so blood sugar levels affect both stamina and behaviour, and this is particularly noticeable in children. When blood sugar increases too rapidly, the body responds by secreting large amounts of insulin, a sugar-lowering hormone. The initial rush of sugar often results in your child becoming restless and irritable, and sometimes hyperactive and aggressive. Then, as the sugar levels plummet, this is followed by tiredness and lack of concentration. This yo-yo effect can be avoided by eating plenty of complex carbohydrates, found in starchy foods such as bread, rice, oats, potatoes and pasta. These provide slow-release energy, because they take longer to be broken down, absorbed and processed by the body, keeping blood sugar levels on a more even keel.

Easy ways to eat more starchy carbohydrates

* Make pasta, rice, bread or potatoes the main part of most meals.
* Add variety by trying lots of different types of bread, including rolls, pittas chapattis, flour tortillas, bagels and breadsticks. Another good source of carbohydrates is rice, such as brown, basmati and risotto, grains such as couscous and quinoa, and pasta and noodles made from other grains such as buckwheat.
* Try serving sweet potatoes, yams or plantains instead of potatoes.
* Encourage children to eat a bowl of wholegrain cereal, without added sugar, as a healthy snack.
* Include some unrefined starchy carbohydrates such as wholewheat bread, and wholewheat pasta occasionally, but remember that unlike adults, children should avoid too many high-fibre foods as they are very filling, which makes it more difficult to fulfil energy needs.

Eat more fruit and vegetables

These are packed with vitamins and minerals and 'phytochemicals', which help to keep the immune system strong and protect against everyday illnesses. To ensure your child gets a wide variety of these nutrients, try to include as many different coloured fruits and vegetables as you can. Both adults and children should aim for at least five portions a day. Fresh, frozen, tinned and dried fruit and vegetables and 100 per cent juice, all count. A child-size portion could be two heaped tablespoons of cooked carrots, peas or sweetcorn, a small apple, pear or banana, three heaped tablespoons of canned fruit salad, a fruity cereal or snack bar, a few dried apricots or a tablespoon of dried fruit such as raisins.

Easy ways to eat more fruit and vegetables

❉ Start the day with a glass of fruit juice at breakfast or top cereals with chopped fresh or dried fruit.

❉ Make your own ice lollies from fresh fruit purée (see page 136).

❉ Serve crunchy vegetable sticks as a snack with favourite dips.

❉ Stir a handful of frozen peas or mixed vegetables into soups and casseroles before serving.

❉ Purée vegetables into sauces or blend with a little stock and milk to make nutritious soups.

❉ Make a pot of 'trail mix' from dried fruit, nuts and seeds to add to lunch boxes and for sprinkling over yoghurts and desserts.

Fibre is the term for indigestible compounds found in whole foods such as wholemeal bread and oats, fruit and vegetables. It is needed to keep your child's digestive system working well and to prevent constipation. Unlike adults, children should avoid very high-fibre foods such as bran-based cereals as these can reduce the absorption of minerals such as iron and calcium. Fruit and vegetables are a much better source of fibre for children.

Eat more calcium and iron-rich foods

Vitamins and minerals are complex substances needed by the body for a whole range of processes. All are important, but of particular note to children are the minerals iron and calcium. Iron, often lacking in children's diets, is needed for both mental and physical development and to make haemoglobin, which transports oxygen around the body. Iron is especially important for girls who need to build up supplies as they approach puberty. Make sure that your child has at least one iron-rich food every day.

Calcium is vital for building strong healthy bones and teeth. It also acts as a 'bone bank', helping to build up bone density from an early age to reduce the risk of osteoporosis later in life. Vitamin D is vital for the absorption and utilisation of calcium. As this vitamin isn't well absorbed from food, the best way for children to get adequate supplies is to spend a few minutes outside everyday, especially on sunny days, but avoid

staying out for long in the middle of the day, when the sun is at its hottest. Encourage your child to eat two portions of calcium-rich food every day. These include a medium-size glass of milk and a carton of yoghurt; or a piece of cheese or tofu, weighing about 25 g (1 oz).

Good sources of iron	Good sources of calcium
Meat, especially beef, lamb and liver	Milk, cheese, yoghurt
Egg yolk	Tinned sardines
Tinned tuna	Broccoli and green leafy vegetables
Dried fruits such as apricots	Tofu and fortified soya milk
Fortified breakfast cereals	White bread

Eat more omega 6 and omega 3

Although we tend to think of all fats as being 'bad', some actually play a protective role in the diet and two in particular are vital: the essential fatty acids (EFAs) known as omega 6 and omega 3. Omega 6 EFAs are involved in the production of prostaglandin, a hormone-like substance needed for healthy cell membranes which has a therapeutic effect on skin problems and allergies. They are found in many oils including sunflower and safflower, soft polyunsaturated margarine, seeds and nuts. Omega 3 EFAs are also found in these oils but additionally include vital substances which come almost solely from fish oils. Vegetarians may get small amounts from flax and pumpkin seeds and leafy green vegetables, although recent evidence suggests that the type of fatty acids found in vegetable sources may not have the same benefits as those in fish. Omega 3 EFAs help to support healthy brain development and there is evidence that they may influence a child's ability to learn and concentrate. Scientists are still studying whether omega 3 can help with conditions such as Attention Deficit Hyperactivity Disorder (ADHD) and other mental illnesses such as depression. Try to make sure that the whole family eats oily fish such as salmon, tuna or sardines at least once a week. If your child refuses to eat fish, there are plenty of polyunsaturated spreads and yoghurt drinks enriched with omega 6 and omega 3.

Eat less sugar

Most children enjoy sugary foods and sweets and eating them occasionally causes no real harm. As children grow older, outside influences will make themselves felt and you will no longer have complete control over what is eaten. A staggering 80 per cent of children eat more added sugars than the maximum level recommended for adults. While sugars occur naturally in foods such as milk and fruit, it's the food containing added sugar that you should try to reduce in your child's diet, including sweets, cookies, cakes and pastries, fizzy and juice drinks. Not only do they contribute to tooth decay, high-sugar foods raise blood sugar levels quickly, causing peaks and troughs of energy. A sugary snack may give your child instant energy, but this will be followed by a dip and these fluctuations in blood sugar levels cause mood swings and affect attentiveness. When checking food labels, watch out for other words for sugar, including sucrose, glucose, fructose, maltose, corn syrup, hydrolysed starch and invert sugar.

Ways to cut down on sugar

* Give your child fewer sugary sweets and snacks. If you can't avoid the sweet shop, encourage better choices such as a small bar of chocolate.
* Instead of sugary juice drinks and canned fizzy drinks such as cola and lemonade, go for unsweetened fruit juice, preferably diluted with water. For a fizzy drink treat, try mixing fruit juice with carbonated water.
* Instead of reaching for the biscuit tin, try serving a brioche roll with a little good-quality jam, crunchy breadsticks or a toasted currant bun.
* Leave the sugar bowl off the breakfast table; sprinkling sugar on cereals should be avoided, as should sugar- and honey-coated kids' cereals.
* Instead of sugary yoghurts, mousses and trifles, offer plain 'bio' or Greek yoghurt with sliced fresh fruit or fruit purée.

Eat less saturated and hydrogenated fats

While adults aspire to eat a high-fibre, low-fat diet, this isn't ideal for children. They need a greater intake of fat than adults as it is a concentrated source of energy. Fat also helps the absorption of vitamins A, D, E and K, as well as calcium. It is, however, important to limit the amount of saturated fats as these raise the type of cholesterol in the blood that increases the risk of coronary heart disease – there is growing evidence that this starts in childhood. From the age of five, children can gradually start to include reduced-fat foods in their diet, such as semi-skimmed/low-fat milk.

Hydrogenation is a process by which liquid oil is turned into solid fat. During the process, trans fats may be formed, which are thought to be more harmful than saturated fats. Always check labels and avoid foods containing hydrogenated fat or hydrogenated vegetable oil.

Ways to cut back on undesirable fats

✳ Limit foods containing high amounts of saturated fats such as butter, cream and foods made with them, including cakes, pastries and cookies.

✳ Cut down on 'visible' fats such as butter on bread, cream on desserts and always trim fat from meats such as chops and bacon.

✳ Choose margarines and spreads that contain little or no hydrogenated or saturated fats.

✳ Avoid fast food takeaways as these are usually fried in partially hydrogenated oil.

✳ Swap fatty snacks for healthy ones some of the time – for example, crunchy breadsticks instead of crisps, a slice of wholemeal toast with jam instead of cookies or a sweet pastry.

Eat less salt

Salt is made up of two components – sodium and chloride. It is sodium which leads to health problems; in excess, it can cause high blood pressure (hypertension), increasing the chances of heart attacks and strokes. It is also linked to an increased risk of osteoporosis and has been shown to aggravate asthma. Children who eat too much salt when young often develop a taste for salty food and will be more likely to continue to eat too much salt when older. Most adults and children eat more than double the recommended daily maximum amount of salt. Children should have considerably less salt than adults.

Maximum daily amount of salt

Age	Max daily salt/sodium intake
1 to 3 years	2 g (0.8 g sodium)
4 to 6 years	3 g (1.2 g sodium)
7 to 10 years	5 g (2 g sodium)
11 and over	6 g (2.5 g sodium)

While obvious solutions include reducing the amount of salt used in cooking and not having extra salt on the table, about three-quarters of the salt we eat is already in the foods we buy. Many processed foods, including some products aimed at children, are high in salt and it's not always the obvious ones. Shop-bought bread, cakes and pastries, baked beans and sauces contain a surprising amount.

Sodium content of everyday foods

Average serving	Sodium (mg)
1 slice of buttered bread	75
Bowl of Rice Crispies cereal	440
Danish pastry	210
Small bag of crisps (25 g/1 oz)	250
Vanilla ice cream	50
Mayonnaise (1 tablespoon)	75
Pickle (1 tablespoon)	565
Soy sauce (1 tablespoon)	1065
Can fizzy drink	20

Some manufacturers have reduced the amount of salt in their products, so it's worth checking carefully when shopping. Most foods are labelled with the amount of sodium (rather than salt) they contain. If you want to compare a product labelled with its salt rather than sodium content, it's worth knowing that there's about 2.5 g of sodium in every 6 g of salt. Other types of sodium are used as preservatives or flavour enhancers, such as monosodium glutamate, often added to processed meats, snacks and soups.

Ways to cut down on salt

✳ Give your child fewer salty foods including salted nuts, bacon, smoked fish and pickles. Don't add a bag of crisps to lunchboxes every day; go for low-salt snacks such as unsalted nuts and home-made popcorn.

✳ Be sparing with sauces, especially bottled and packet sauces, soy sauce, Worcestershire sauce, brown sauce and tomato ketchup. If you use these when cooking, reduce or omit additional salt.

✳ Make your own stock or choose lower-salt stock cubes and use herbs and spices to add flavour to cooking.

✳ Choose tinned vegetables and pulses without added salt.

✳ Compare labels to help you choose those with less added salt. Similar products often vary considerably in the amount of sodium they contain.

- Ask for unsalted fries and chips when eating out in restaurants or buying takeaways and make them an occasional treat only.
- Replace processed meats such as burgers and sausages with home-made versions.
- Do not use salt at the table. Always taste your food before automatically adding extra salt and encourage your children to do the same.

Understanding food labels

Food labels are a useful source of information, but don't assume that a product labelled as 'lower in fat' is necessarily a healthy choice; in many products, fat or sugar may still be high. Ingredients are placed in order of quantity, so if sugar or fat comes near the top of the list you know the food contains a lot of these. 'Traffic light' labelling is used on a growing number of foods and in many supermarkets. They enable you to see at a glance if the product has high, medium or low amounts of fat, saturated fat, sugars and salt. In addition, you can also see the amount of these nutrients in a serving of the food. As a general guide:

- Foods that contain 15 g of sugar or more per 100 g are high in sugar; low is 5 g or less per 100 g.
- Foods that contain 20 g of fat or more per 100 g (5 g of saturates or more per 100 g) are high in fat; low is 3 g or less per 100 g (1 g of saturates or less per 100 g).
- Foods that contain 0.5 g of sodium or more per 100 g are high in sodium; 0.1 g or less per 100 g is considered a low amount.

You should also check labels for cheap 'bulking' ingredients, often used by manufacturers to keep production costs low. These include modified starch, modified cornflour and maltodextrin, and have little or no nutritional value. Also check labels for 'mechanically separated beef, pork or chicken'. This is the meat residue left when all the prime cuts have been removed and is usually pressure-blasted off the bones forming a pink-coloured slurry. It is often formed into shaped meat products such as 'nuggets'.

The negative health effects of children consuming large amounts of additives including preservatives and artificial flavourings, colourings and sweeteners is still being researched, but it is likely that there is a connection between some children's behavioural problems and their diet. Certain additives such as sulphur dioxide, which may be used in dried fruit destroys vitamins and can cause asthma attacks in susceptible children. Other food additives which children should avoid if possible are:

❋ E210, benzoic acid
❋ E211, sodium benzoate
❋ E250, sodium nitrite
❋ E251, sodium nitrate
❋ E252, potassium nitrate (saltpetre)
❋ E310, propyl gallate
❋ E312, dodecyl gallate
❋ E320, butylated hydroxyanisole
❋ E321, butylated hydroxytolene (BHT)
❋ E621, monosodium glutamate
❋ E627, sodium guanylate (guanosine)
❋ E631, inosine 5
❋ E635, sodium 5

Dealing with food allergies

Allergies and intolerances to certain foods vary in severity. They are actually two very different problems, yet the symptoms are similar. An allergy is an inappropriate response by the body's immune system to what should be a harmless food, whereas food intolerance is the inability to digest certain foods. If your child frequently has one or more of the following symptoms after eating, you should consult your doctor:

❋ Nausea, abdominal pain, bloating, vomiting or diarrhoea.
❋ Swelling of the face, mouth or tongue.
❋ Wheeziness, streaming eyes and sneezing.
❋ Blotchy rashes, particularly on the face.

Foods that can bring on allergies include nuts, seeds, fish and shellfish, egg white, berries and citrus fruit. Nuts (especially peanuts and brazils) are the most common of these and some schools ban these from all packed lunches to protect those children who may react even if they are only in the vicinity of nuts. Children under the age of three with a family history of allergy should not be given nuts in any form. Some children may have a severe (anaphylactic) reaction to certain foods, manifesting itself as difficulty with breathing, a very fast pulse rate and bluish skin or lips. In these cases immediate hospital treatment should be sought.

Food intolerances may be present at birth or may develop later. Lactose intolerance is the inability to digest the sugars in cow's milk. If your child suffers from this it will be necessary to follow a dairy-free diet in which soya or low-lactose milk products are used instead. Avoid foods labelled as containing milk, butter, margarine, cheese, yoghurt, cream, whey, casein/caseinates and lactose. If avoiding dairy products you will need to ensure an adequate intake of calcium and vitamins A and D.

Coeliac disease is a sensitivity to gluten, a protein found in cereals, including wheat, rye, barley and oats (it is also possible to have an intolerance just to wheat). More common in girls than boys, it often runs in families and can start at any age. It affects about one person in 130. There are many gluten-free products available, including breads and pasta.

Preventing obesity

It is important to be aware of your child's weight and eating habits as children who are obese may have social and psychological as well as physical problems. However, you should also bear in mind that like adults, children come in all shapes and sizes. Many pre-adolescent children, particularly girls, are slightly plump; children often gain weight before a growth spurt and as long as they are healthy and active, this is nothing to worry about. Make sure that your child starts the day with a good breakfast and takes a healthy snack for break-time, if allowed. After school, when children are often ravenous, offer fruit and starchy snacks such as a lightly buttered roll or toast before the demands for cookies and crisps start. Finally, make a healthy main meal for the whole family; you cannot expect your children to eat well if you don't.

Although eating disorders such as anorexia nervosa (voluntary starvation) and bulimia (alternate starving, bingeing and vomiting) occur mainly in teenagers, they are increasing affecting much younger children. Some early signs include a sudden desire to follow a faddish diet, making excuses not to join family meals, or obsessive exercising. If your child is displaying signs of an eating disorder, medical help is essential; don't try to treat it yourself.

Help prevent eating disorders by

✢ Avoiding constant discussions about slimming diets in the home and over-criticising your child's eating habits. Instead, encourage a healthy attitude towards food.
✢ Build up your child's self-esteem.
✢ Balance the media portrayal of thinness with a more realistic one.

The best way to ensure your child gets the necessary nutrients for good health and avoids foods which are high in saturated fats, salt, sugar and additives, is to prepare the food yourself, using fresh, good-quality ingredients. The recipes in this book will show you how to improve your child's eating habits without spending hours in the kitchen. All are simple to prepare and will appeal to children and adults alike.

breakfast

There's nothing quite as good as waking up to the aroma of freshly baked muffins! These muffins are really quick to make and the dry and wet ingredients can be measured out the night before, ready to mix together and bake.

Blueberry muffins

MAKES 9

225 g (2 cups) self-raising flour

1 tsp baking powder

Pinch of salt

150 g (⅔ cup) light brown sugar

50 g (½ cup) porridge (rolled) oats

1 egg, lightly beaten

300 ml (1¼ cups) semi-skimmed milk

1 tsp vanilla extract

6 Tbsp sunflower oil

150 g (1¼ cups) fresh blueberries

2 tsp icing (confectioners') sugar, preferably unrefined

✳ Preheat the oven to 190 °C/375 °F/gas 5. Lightly grease a 9-cup muffin tin or line with paper muffin cases.

✳ Put the flour, baking powder, salt and sugar in a large bowl and stir together. In another bowl, mix together the oats, egg, milk, vanilla and oil. Leave to soak for at least 10 minutes (the oats will absorb some of the liquid and thicken the mixture), or overnight in the refrigerator if preferred.

✳ When ready to bake, stir the blueberries into the wet ingredients, then add this mixture to the dry ingredients and stir briefly until just mixed together, but still a little lumpy.

✳ Divide evenly between the muffin cups or cases, then bake for about 20 minutes, or until well-risen, golden-brown and firm to the touch. Allow the muffins to cool in the tin for 10 minutes, before removing. Lightly dust the tops with icing sugar and serve warm.

Variation: *For mixed fruit muffins, use 75 g (½ cup) dried fruits such as sultanas (golden raisins) or raisins, blueberries or cherries, or chopped apricots. Add them to the oat mixture when soaking, plus an extra tablespoon of milk, to soften and plump them up a little before baking.*

Nutritional note: *Rolled oats are whole oat grains which have had the husks removed and are then rolled flat. They contain all the nutrients of the whole grain including B vitamins, which are needed for the release of energy from carbohydrates.*

Some children find boiled eggs difficult to tackle and fried eggs can be greasy, so here an egg is cracked into a small dish and cooked with just a little crème fraîche.

Creamy egg pot

SERVES 1

1 egg

Butter or sunflower margarine, to grease

Salt and freshly ground black pepper (optional)

2 tsp crème fraîche

Buttered fingers of wholemeal toast, to serve

* Lightly grease the inside of a cocotte dish or ramekin with butter or margarine. Crack the egg into the dish and sprinkle the top with a little salt and pepper, if liked. Spoon the crème fraîche on top of the egg.
* Cover the top of the dish with foil and place in a small saucepan. Pour in enough boiling water to come two-thirds up the dish. Cover the pan with a lid and simmer for 7–8 minutes, depending how well you want the egg cooked. Carefully lift the dish out of the water and serve with hot buttered wholemeal toast.

Tip: *It's best to keep eggs in their box in a cold refrigerator. Use them as close to the packing date as possible and always within the 'best before' date. Avoid cracked or dirty eggs.*

Nutritional note: *Look out for omega 3-rich eggs, especially if your child won't eat oily fish. These come from chickens that are fed on omega 3 polyunsaturated fatty-acid-enriched feed.*

Shop-bought granola and crunchy-type breakfast cereals can be very high in sugar and additives. Making your own gives you more control over these and allows you to adjust the mixture to include your child's favourite fruits and nuts.

Crunchy granola cereal

MAKES 6 SERVINGS

175 g (1¾ cups) porridge (rolled) oats

50 g (⅔ cup) desiccated (shredded) coconut

50 g (½ cup) chopped hazelnuts

2 Tbsp sesame seeds

25 g (2 Tbsp) light brown sugar

100 ml (scant ½ cup) water

2 Tbsp clear honey

1 tsp finely grated orange rind

100 ml (scant ½ cup) sunflower oil

75 g (½ cup) sultanas (golden raisins)

Semi-skimmed milk, yoghurt or fruit juice, to serve

✱ Preheat the oven to 190 °C/375 °F/gas 5. Put the oats, coconut, hazelnuts, sesame seeds and half the sugar in a large bowl and mix together. Whisk the remaining sugar and water together in a jug, until dissolved. Add the honey, orange rind and oil to the jug and whisk again. Drizzle over the dry ingredients, then mix together evenly with your hands.

✱ Spread the mixture out on a non-stick baking tray and bake for 25–30 minutes, turning the pieces once or twice during cooking, so that they brown evenly. Remove from the oven and allow to cool completely. Mix in the sultanas and store in an airtight container for up to two weeks. Serve with milk, yoghurt or fruit juice.

Tip: *Adjust this tasty granola to your child's tastes; chopped dried apricots, peaches, apples, cranberries or blueberries all work well. Don't just limit this nutritious treat to breakfast-time; it makes a great snack when ravenous children arrive home from school and is also good as a topping for yoghurt desserts.*
Nutritional note: *Hazelnuts and sesame seeds are good sources of vitamin E – great for the skin and hair. Vitamin E also strengthens the immune system and is an antioxidant, protecting cell membranes.*

Smoothies make a great 'meal in a glass' and are ideal for children who can't face a big breakfast. Bananas are good energy boosters and as long as they are well-ripened, this smoothie needs no additional sugar or sweetener.

Get-up-and-go banana smoothie

SERVES 1

1 medium banana, peeled and sliced

4 Tbsp Greek yoghurt

225 ml (1 cup) semi-skimmed milk, chilled

½ tsp vanilla extract

A few ice cubes or crushed ice (optional), to serve

✳ Put the sliced banana, yoghurt and half the milk in a blender and process for about 1 minute until smooth.

✳ Add the remaining milk and vanilla, then process for a few more seconds until smooth and frothy. Put the ice in a tall glass, if using. Pour the smoothie over the ice and serve immediately.

Variations: *For a chocolate banana smoothie, add 1–2 teaspoons of drinking chocolate when blending the banana.*
✳ For a honey-berry smoothie, use 75 g (½ cup) raspberries, strawberries or blueberries (or a combination) and 1–2 teaspoons of clear honey (depending on the ripeness of the fruit) instead of the banana and vanilla. Add the yoghurt and milk, as above.
✳ For a tropical smoothie, use the flesh of half a ripe mango and half a banana, and add the yoghurt and milk as above.
Tip: *Try to avoid flavoured milkshake syrups or powders as these are usually high in both sugar and additives.*
Nutritional note: *Bananas are rich in potassium, a mineral often lacking in diets high in processed foods. They make a great snack before or after sporting activities as potassium is vital for the proper functioning of muscles. A deficiency may lead to fatigue and insomnia.*

This light omelette makes breakfast-time special and is delicious filled with mushrooms, as here, or you could fill with a spoonful of good-quality conserve, for a sweet version.

Fluffy omelette with mushrooms

SERVES 1–2

15 g (1 Tbsp) butter or sunflower margarine

50 g (2 oz) button mushrooms, sliced

2 eggs, separated

1 Tbsp cold water

Salt and freshly ground black (optional)

1 tsp sunflower oil

Buttered bread or toast, to serve

❋ Melt half the butter or margarine in a small non-stick frying or omelette pan. Add the mushrooms and cook over a medium heat for 4–5 minutes, stirring occasionally until just tender but not browned. Tip onto a plate and set aside.

❋ Beat the egg yolks and water together with a little salt and pepper, if liked. Whisk the egg whites until stiff, then fold into the egg yolks using a metal spoon. Preheat the grill to medium.

❋ Melt the remaining butter and oil in the pan and pour in the egg mixture. Cook over a gentle heat for 3 minutes, until the underside is golden-brown. Scatter over the mushrooms, then cook under the grill for a further 2–3 minutes until the top is golden. Serve straight away with buttered bread or toast.

Tip: *Check that eggs are really fresh by placing in a bowl of cold water; they should stay at the bottom; less fresh eggs will bob up a bit and stale ones will float.*
Nutritional note: *Eggs are a highly nutritious food and provide a wide range of essential nutrients. As well as high-quality protein, they contain useful amounts of vitamins, minerals and lecithin, an important 'brain food' which contributes to concentration and memory. A single medium-sized egg contains about 6 g (¼ oz) of protein (nearly a third of a six-year-old and a quarter of a ten-year-old's daily requirement).*

Many versions of this popular and delicious bake are high in both sugar and fat. This one is made with sunflower oil rather than butter and contains a mixture of wholemeal and white flours, yet still has a lovely light, moist texture.

Banana breakfast bread

MAKES 10 SLICES

125 g (1 cup) self-raising flour

125 g (1 cup) self-raising wholemeal flour

1 tsp ground cinnamon

75 g (⅔ cup) walnuts or pecans, roughly chopped (optional)

125 g (½ cup) light brown sugar

150 ml (⅔ cup) sunflower oil

3 eggs, lightly beaten

2 large ripe bananas, about 400 g (14 oz) in total, weighed with their skins on

Finely grated rind and juice of ½ orange

❉ Preheat the oven to 180 °C/350 °F/gas 4. Lightly grease a 900-g (2-lb) loaf tin and line the bottom with baking parchment. Sift the flours and cinnamon into a large bowl, adding any bran left in the sieve. Stir in the nuts.

❉ In another bowl, beat the sugar and oil together until combined. Beat in the eggs a little at a time. In another bowl, mash the bananas with the orange rind and juice until smooth, then beat into the sugar, oil and egg mixture. With a large metal spoon, carefully fold the banana mixture into the flour mixture, until just combined.

❉ Spoon the mixture into the prepared tin. Bake for 50 minutes, or until well-risen and firm to the touch. Leave in the tin for 10 minutes, then turn out onto a wire rack and peel off the lining paper. When cool, wrap in greaseproof paper, then in foil and store in the refrigerator. Serve cut into thick slices spread with a little jam, if liked.

Tip: *Make sure that the bananas are really ripe for maximum flavour and sweetness.*
Nutritional note: *Sunflower oil is a great provider of good-for-you polyunsaturated fats and contains almost no undesirable saturated fat.*

A steaming hot bowl of oatmeal is the perfect start to a cold winter day, but this dish may also be served chilled in warmer weather.

Creamed oatmeal with peaches

SERVES 2

125 g (⅔ cup) dried peaches

125 ml (½ cup) apple juice

1 Tbsp clear honey

65 g (½ cup) rolled oats

450 ml (1¾ cups) semi-skimmed milk

Greek yoghurt (optional), to serve

✻ Chop the dried peaches into small pieces and put in a bowl with the apple juice and honey. Stir, then cover and leave to soak overnight in the refrigerator.

✻ Put the oats in a heavy-based saucepan. Add the milk and slowly bring to the boil. Simmer for 3–4 minutes (or according to packet instructions), stirring frequently.

✻ Divide the oatmeal between two bowls and serve each topped with the soaked peaches and a little Greek yoghurt, if liked.

Variation: *For chilled oatmeal, leave to cool, stirring occasionally. Stir in 150 ml (⅔ cup) Greek yoghurt and chill for at least one hour, or overnight. Serve chilled with the soaked peaches, chopped fresh or canned fruit or 1–2 tablespoons of sweetened fruit purée.*

Nutritional note: *Oats have a low glycaemic index, which means they are digested and absorbed slowly, producing a gentle rise in blood glucose levels. This will give sustained energy to keep children alert until lunchtime.*

As waffle irons need little or no greasing, waffles are only unhealthy if served smothered with butter and syrup! Because the batter contains raising agent, it needs to be made just before using to guarantee a light, airy texture.

Cinnamon waffles

SERVES 4 (MAKES ABOUT 8 WAFFLES)

150 g (1¼ cups) plain (all-purpose) flour

1 tsp baking powder

½ tsp ground cinnamon

1 Tbsp caster (superfine) sugar

1 large egg, separated

200 ml (¾ cup) semi-skimmed milk

15 g (1 Tbsp) butter, melted

Maple syrup, to serve

�֍ Prepare and preheat the waffle iron or maker according to the manufacturer's instructions. Meanwhile, sift the flour, baking powder, cinnamon and sugar into a mixing bowl and make a well in the centre. Add the egg yolk and milk and gradually work into the flour using a whisk. Stir in the melted butter.

�֍ In a clean, grease-free bowl, whisk the egg white until stiff, then gently fold it into the batter with a large metal spoon.

✖ Spoon enough batter into the middle of the hot waffle iron to cover the lower plates sufficiently, then close the lid tightly. If you are using a waffle iron on the hob, cook for 30–45 seconds, then turn over and cook for a further 30 seconds, or until the waffle is golden brown on both sides. If you are using an electric waffle maker, follow the manufacturer's instructions.

✖ When the waffles are ready, carefully remove them, taking care not to scratch the non-stick coating. Keep them warm on a wire cooling rack covered with a clean tea towel while cooking the remaining waffles. Serve hot, drizzled with a little maple syrup.

Variations: *For pecan waffles, stir 25 g (¼ cup) finely chopped pecan nuts into the mixture when adding the melted butter.*
✖ For chocolate waffles, substitute 2 tablespoons of cocoa powder for 2 tablespoons of the flour and add an extra teaspoon of sugar to the mixture.

Bought jams and conserves often have a low fruit content and a huge amount of added sugar. This healthy alternative is simple to make and deliciously fruity.

Apricot spread

MAKES ABOUT 350 G (1 CUP)

225 g (1⅓ cups) dried apricots

450 ml (1¾ cups) water

2 tsp vanilla extract

✳ Put the apricots in a saucepan and pour over just enough of the water to cover them. Slowly bring to the boil, then cover the pan and gently simmer for 25–30 minutes, or until the apricots are very soft. Check and stir the mixture occasionally towards the end of cooking time and add a little more of the water if it seems to be getting too dry.

✳ Turn off the heat and leave the mixture, still covered, for about 10 minutes to allow it to cool a little. Spoon the cooked fruit into a food processor or blender and add the remaining water and vanilla extract. Blend to a smooth thick purée.

✳ Spoon the apricot spread into a clean jar or container and leave to cool completely. Cover and keep in the refrigerator for up to ten days.

Tips: *As well as a spread for bread and toast, try a spoonful on top of plain yoghurt or porridge. You can also dilute it with a tiny amount of fruit juice or water and use as a sauce for ice cream or a sponge pudding.*
✳ *Ideally, the jar or container should be sterilised before adding the spread. The simplest way to do this is to clean it in a hot dishwasher cycle before use.*
Variations: *Make an apricot and apple spread by using apple juice instead of water, or an apricot and orange spread with orange juice. For both variations, leave out the vanilla extract.*
✳ *For a more exotic flavour, substitute dried mangoes and pineapple for some of the apricots and flavour with 1 teaspoon of orange flower or rosewater.*

Cookies for breakfast may not sound like a good idea, but these protein-packed bakes make a great start to the day if served with a glass of milk or some yoghurt and fresh fruit.

Peanut butter cookies

MAKES 20

175 g (⅔ cup) crunchy peanut butter (with no added sugar)

50 g (¼ cup) unsalted butter, at room temperature

50 g (¼ cup) golden caster (superfine) sugar

40 g (3 Tbsp) light brown sugar

1 egg, lightly beaten

125 g (1 cup) self-raising flour

50 g (2 cups) cornflakes, lightly crushed

✳ Preheat the oven to 180 °C/375 °F/gas 5. Line two baking sheets with baking parchment. Put the peanut butter and butter in a large bowl and beat together until well-mixed and creamy. Add the sugars and beat again. Gradually add the egg, a little at a time, beating well after each addition. Sift over the flour and mix to a stiff dough.

✳ Put the crushed cornflakes on a plate. Roll the cookie dough into walnut-sized balls, then roll in the cornflakes to coat. Place on the prepared baking sheets, spacing them slightly apart, then flatten them a little with the palm of your hand (this will stop them rolling off the sheet)!

✳ Bake for 10–12 minutes until firm, then remove from the oven and transfer to a wire rack to cool. Store in an airtight container for up to a week. Serve two or three cookies with a glass of milk, a smoothie or a small bowl of yoghurt and fresh fruit.

Tip: *Making your own peanut butter is quick and easy: blend 175 g (⅔ cup) unsalted roasted shelled peanuts for a few seconds in a blender or food processor, until roughly chopped. Drizzle 2 tablespoons of groundnut or sunflower oil over the top and add a small pinch of salt, if liked. Process for about 30 seconds for crunchy peanut butter and 1–2 minutes for smooth.* **Nutritional note:** *Peanut butter is a good source of protein. Just 50 g (3 Tbsp) will provide about a quarter of a child's daily requirement.*

These high-energy bars are perfect for a mid-morning snack or when there isn't time for breakfast. They also make a great addition to lunchboxes.

Brunch bars

MAKES 12

250 g (2½ cups) rolled oats

125 g (⅔ cup) dried apricots, finely chopped

75 g (½ cup) raisins

75 g (½ cup) almonds, roughly chopped

50 g (½ cup) ground almonds

50 g (⅓ cup) sesame seeds

50 g (⅓ cup) plain or milk chocolate drops

150 g (⅔ cup) butter

200 g (1 cup) demerara sugar

150 g (½ cup) clear honey

✤ Preheat the oven to 190 °C/375 °F/gas 5. Grease and line the base of a 23-cm (9-in) square tin with baking parchment. Put the oats, dried fruit, nuts, seeds and chocolate drops in bowl and mix together.

✤ Gently heat the butter, sugar and honey in a saucepan, stirring occasionally until the sugar has melted. Turn up the heat a little and simmer for 4 minutes. Pour the melted mixture over the dry ingredients and mix together thoroughly.

✤ Spoon the mixture into the prepared tin and bake for 20 minutes, until just turning golden. Place the tin on a cooling rack and leave until completely cold, then chill in the refrigerator for 2 hours. Turn out onto a board and cut into 14 bars. Store in an airtight container, interleaved with baking parchment.

Tip: *The bars can be successfully frozen by wrapping each individually in clingfilm or foil. They will keep in the freezer for up to three months. For lunchboxes, they can be packed frozen and will have defrosted by lunchtime.*
Nutritional note: *Of all nuts, almonds contain the most calcium, vital for growing bones and healthy teeth. Although packed with nutrients, these breakfast bars have a fairly high fat content, so don't leave them in the cookie jar where they may all be eaten in one go!*

Although its name suggests otherwise, buttermilk is very low in fat and gives these mini pancakes a lovely light texture. They are delicious served with thick yoghurt and a drizzle of maple syrup or honey.

Buttermilk pancakes

**SERVES 2–3
(MAKES 6 PANCAKES)**

125 g (1 cup)
self-raising flour

Pinch of salt

15 g (1 Tbsp) caster
(superfine) sugar

1 large egg, separated

150 ml (⅔ cup)
buttermilk

2 tsp sunflower oil

Thick yoghurt and
maple syrup or
honey, to serve

✳ Sift the flour and salt into a mixing bowl. Stir in the sugar. Make a well in the centre, add the egg yolk and buttermilk, and gradually work into the flour using a whisk. In a clean, grease-free bowl, whisk the egg white until stiff, then gently fold it into the batter with a large metal spoon.

✳ Heat a griddle or a large, heavy, non-stick frying pan, then lightly grease with a teaspoon of the oil. Spoon large, heaped spoonfuls of the batter into the hot pan – you should be able to cook three pancakes at a time. Cook for 2–3 minutes, until the underneath is lightly browned, then turn over and cook the other side for a further 2 minutes. Remove from the pan and keep warm while making the remaining pancakes, adding the remaining oil to the pan. Serve drizzled with honey or maple syrup and a spoonful of yoghurt.

Variation: *For wholemeal banana pancakes, make the batter using wholemeal self-raising flour and an extra tablespoon of milk and fold a small sliced banana into the mixture. If liked, add a few sultanas (golden raisins) or raisins, too.*
Tip: *Buttermilk was traditionally created from the liquid left over after the creamy part of the milk had been churned into butter, but these days it is more likely to be made by adding a culture to skimmed milk. If you have problems finding buttermilk, add half a teaspoon of lemon juice to 150 ml (⅔ cup) semi-skimmed milk and leave it to stand at room temperature for about 15 minutes before using.*
Nutritional note: *Buttermilk is a good source of calcium and phosphorus, both of which are essential for healthy bones and teeth. It contains only 0.1% fat.*

Known in France as 'pain perdu' (lost bread), this is a great way to get children to eat eggs. Traditionally served sprinkled with cinnamon sugar, it could also be topped with a little low-sugar jam or with a drizzle of maple syrup and crisp bacon.

French toast

SERVES 1

Two slices wholemeal or white bread, preferably a day or two old

1 egg

2 tsp semi-skimmed milk

Small knob of unsalted butter

1 tsp caster (superfine) sugar

Pinch of ground cinnamon

✳ If liked, trim the crusts off the bread, then cut each slice in half. Crack the egg onto a plate, add the milk and lightly beat together with a fork.

✳ Melt the butter in a heavy-based non-stick frying pan and swirl around the base. When it starts to sizzle, dip the pieces of bread in the egg mixture on both sides, then quickly add to the pan. Cook for 1–2 minutes until golden-brown and crisp, then turn over and cook for a further minute.

✳ Meanwhile, blend the sugar and cinnamon together. Remove the French toast from the pan and sprinkle with cinnamon sugar. Allow to cool for a minute before serving.

Variation: *For savoury French toast, grill two rashers of trimmed lean, unsmoked back or streaky bacon for 2–3 minutes on each side until lightly browned and cooked through (or dry-fry in the frying pan before cooking the French toast). Drain well. Serve on top of the French toast and drizzle with 1 teaspoon of maple syrup before serving, if liked.*

Nutritional notes: *Eggs provide high-quality protein – protein that contains all eight of the essential amino acids, vital for growth and development.*

✳ *Shallow-frying needn't be an unhealthy method of cooking providing you use a good non-stick pan and the minimum amount of fat.*

Ripe fresh fruits are the simplest start to the day and provide plenty of vital vitamins. Serve with yoghurt for protein and follow with a slice of wholemeal toast or a couple of rice cakes to add some starchy carbohydrates.

Green fruit salad

SERVES 4

2 tsp caster (superfine) sugar

100 ml (scant ½ cup) cold water

2 Tbsp lime cordial

125 g (¾ cup) green seedless grapes

2 kiwi fruit, peeled and sliced

1 green apple, quartered, cored and cut into bite-sized pieces

1 small ripe Galia or Ogen melon, halved, de-seeded, peeled and cut into bite-sized pieces

Natural or Greek yoghurt, to serve

✳ Whisk the sugar and water in a jug with a fork until dissolved, then stir in the lime cordial.

✳ Put the prepared fruit in a serving bowl and pour over the syrup. Toss well to coat the fruit, then serve straight away or cover and keep in the refrigerator for up to 12 hours. For maximum flavour, serve at room temperature or just slightly chilled, accompanied by a dollop of yoghurt.

Tip: *Leave out the sugar if the fruit is really ripe and sweet. If you don't want to buy lime cordial, use the juice of a lime instead, adjusting the sugar if necessary.*
Variation: *For winter fruits in ginger syrup, chop 300 g (1¾ cups) mixed dried fruits such as apples, peaches and apricots into bite-sized pieces. Put in a saucepan with 600 ml (2½ cups) apple juice or water and 3 tablespoons of ginger syrup form a jar of preserved ginger. Slowly bring to the boil, then remove from the heat and leave to cool. Transfer to a bowl, cover and chill in the refrigerator overnight.*
Nutritional note: *Children and adults alike should aim to eat five portions of fruit and vegetables daily and starting the day with a delicious fruit salad makes this much easier to achieve.*

lunch

These mini pizzas are really quick to prepare and cook, so are ideal if you've been out all morning but still want to serve a hot, healthy lunch.

Mini pizza grills

SERVES 4

4 English white or wholemeal muffins or bread rolls about 12 cm (5 in) across

25 g (2 Tbsp) polyunsaturated margarine

1 Tbsp sun-dried tomato paste

½ tsp dried oregano or mixed herbs

Salt and freshly ground black pepper

200 g (7 oz) mozzarella cheese, thinly sliced

1 Peperami (pepperoni) salami stick, thinly sliced

1 small red or yellow (bell) pepper, halved, de-seeded and cut into thin strips

4 cherry tomatoes, halved

❊ Preheat the grill to medium. Grill the muffins or baps for about 1 minute on each side until golden brown, then cut in half horizontally using a serrated knife. Grill the cut sides for about 30 seconds until the surface is dry, but not coloured.

❊ Blend together the margarine, tomato paste, herbs and a little salt and pepper, to taste. Spread over the cut sides of the muffins or baps. Arrange the mozzarella on the muffins, top with the Peperami and red or yellow pepper, then place a cherry tomato half in the middle of each, cut-side up. Cook under the grill for 4–5 minutes, until the cheese is melted and bubbling and the vegetables lightly browned. Cool for a minute before serving (melted cheese can be very hot).

Variation: *Thick slices of day-old ciabatta can be used instead of the muffins or baps.*
Nutritional note: *Red (bell) peppers are an excellent source of beta-carotene and vitamin C. Both these nutrients are powerful antioxidants, which can help protect your child against illness and disease.*

These light-textured tasty cheese nuggets coated with crispy crumbs are served with a smooth tomato sauce with just a hint of sweet and sour flavour.

Cheese bites in rich tomato sauce

SERVES 4

For the tomato sauce

2 Tbsp olive oil

1 small red onion, peeled and roughly chopped

400-g (14-oz) tin chopped tomatoes

1 tsp red wine vinegar

1 tsp light brown sugar

1 Tbsp soy sauce

For the cheese bites

100 g (2 cups) fresh white breadcrumbs

1 Tbsp plain (all-purpose) flour

225 g (8 oz) Cheddar cheese, finely grated

Salt and freshly ground black pepper, to taste

2 egg whites

2 Tbsp olive oil

✱ Start by making the sauce. Heat the oil in a small saucepan and gently cook the onion for 10 minutes, until soft. Add the remaining sauce ingredients, bring to the boil, cover and simmer gently for 10 minutes. Allow to cool slightly, then purée in a blender or food processor until smooth. Return the sauce to the saucepan.

✱ While the sauce is cooking, prepare the cheese bites. Put 75 g (1½ cups) of the breadcrumbs, the flour and cheese in a mixing bowl. Season with salt and pepper and mix well. In a separate bowl, whisk the egg whites until stiff but not dry, then fold into the cheese mixture, a third at a time. Shape into 20 balls, then roll in the remaining breadcrumbs to coat them.

✱ Heat 1 tablespoon of oil in a large frying pan over a medium heat. Add half the cheese bites and gently cook for 4–5 minutes, turning frequently until golden all over. Remove from the pan with a slotted spoon, place on kitchen paper and keep warm. Cook the remaining cheese bites in the rest of the oil. While the second batch is cooking, reheat the sauce until it is gently bubbling. Serve the cheese bites with the tomato sauce and some steamed green beans and peas, if liked.

Tip: *Use the egg yolks in another recipe, such as Vanilla ice cream (see page 132).*
Nutritional note: *While we should all eat a minimal amount of fried food, children need a higher proportion of fat than adults in their diet, so it's fine to use this method of cooking occasionally. Use a good quality non-stick frying pan, which reduces the amount of oil needed, and cook in sunflower, rapeseed or olive oil, which contains the antioxidant vitamin E and healthy monusaturated fats.*

Smooth puréed soups are sometimes more popular with children than those with 'bits' and can encourage them to eat more vegetables. Serve with crunchy cheese croutons and they'll be clamouring for more.

Creamy vegetable soup

SERVES 4

For the soup

15 g (1 Tbsp) polyunsaturated margarine

1 small onion, peeled and finely chopped

1 garlic clove, peeled and crushed

450 ml (1¾ cups) vegetable stock

1 large carrot, peeled and roughly chopped

1 medium potato, about 150 g (5½ oz), peeled and roughly chopped

½ small sweet potato, about 150 g (5½ oz), peeled and roughly chopped

2–3 sprigs of broccoli

1 Tbsp tomato paste

150 ml (⅔ cup) semi-skimmed milk

1 Tbsp chopped fresh parsley (optional)

Salt and freshly ground black pepper, to taste

For the cheese croutons

3 slices wholemeal or white bread

15 g (1 Tbsp) polyunsaturated margarine, softened

25 g (1 oz) mild or medium Cheddar, finely grated

Tip: *If you prefer a chunkier texture, cut the carrot, potato and sweet potato into 1-cm (½-in) dice and the broccoli into tiny florets. Simmer for 10 minutes, then purée just half the soup and return to the pan with the unpuréed soup.*
Nutritional note: *Choose sweet potatoes with bright orange flesh for this recipe. They're packed with antioxidant carotenoids, such as betacarotene, which help to boost and protect the immune system.*

✳ Start by making the soup. Melt the margarine in a large saucepan, preferably non-stick, and gently cook the onion for 8–10 minutes, or until tender. Add the garlic and cook for a few seconds more, then pour in the stock and bring to the boil. Add the remaining prepared vegetables to the pan. Turn down the heat until the soup is gently simmering, then half-cover with a lid and cook for 12 minutes, or until the vegetables are very tender. Remove from the heat and stir in the tomato paste.

✳ While the soup is simmering, prepare the croutons. Preheat the oven to 180 °C/350 °F/gas 4.

Butter the bread, then trim off the crusts. Sprinkle the buttered bread with cheese and press down gently with the palm of your hand. Using a sharp knife, cut into 1-cm (½-in) cubes and place them, cheese-side up, on a baking sheet. Bake for 15 minutes, until golden-brown and crisp.

✳ Ladle the soup into a food processor or liquidiser and blend until very smooth. Return the soup to the pan, stir in the milk and parsley, if using, season to taste and reheat until piping hot. Serve with the croutons.

A warming soup served with crusty bread or soft buttered buns, makes a filling lunch or supper dish. This brightly coloured carrot soup is enriched with red lentils which help to thicken the stock.

Carrot and lentil soup

SERVES 4

25 g (2 Tbsp) polyunsaturated margarine

1 medium leek, washed and thinly sliced

3 Tbsp red lentils

450 g (1 lb) carrots, peeled and sliced

½ tsp ground coriander

600 ml (2½ cups) hot vegetable stock

About 300 ml (1¼ cups) semi-skimmed milk

Salt and freshly ground black pepper

Natural yoghurt (optional), to serve

❄ Melt the margarine in a large heavy-based saucepan. Add the leek, cover the pan and cook gently for 5 minutes, or until it begins to soften, but not colour. Stir in the lentils, carrots and coriander and cook for 2–3 minutes, stirring frequently. Pour in the stock and bring to the boil. Reduce the heat, cover and simmer for about 20 minutes, or until all the ingredients are tender.

❄ Leave the soup to cool slightly, then purée in a blender or food processor until very smooth. Return the soup to the pan and add enough milk to make the soup the consistency you require. Season to taste with salt and pepper and reheat gently until piping hot, but not boiling. Ladle into bowls (warm those for adults, first) and serve with a swirl of yoghurt on the top, if liked.

Tip: *For a more substantial soup, add a small potato cut into chunks with the carrots and scatter some grated Cheddar or red Leicester cheese over the top when serving.*

Nutritional note: *Lentils have an impressive range of nutrients, especially the minerals iron and zinc, vital for young and adolescent children. Low in fat, lentils are rich in protein, so whenever you can, add a tablespoonful or two to dishes such as soups and casseroles.*

Here, slices of tomato, courgettes and peppers (or your child's favourite vegetables) are topped with a cheese- and egg-enriched scone mixture, then baked. When turned out it makes a delicious pizza as the vegetables are kept moist and tender.

Upside-down pizza

SERVES 2–3

- 1 tomato
- ½ yellow (bell) pepper, halved and de-seeded
- 1 small courgette (zucchini)
- 25 g (1 oz) Peperami (pepperoni) salami stick
- 50 g (½ cup) wholemeal flour
- 50 g (½ cup) self-raising flour
- ½ tsp baking powder
- Pinch of salt
- 15 g (1 Tbsp) butter or polyunsaturated margarine
- 50 g (2 oz) medium Cheddar cheese, grated
- 1 egg
- 1 Tbsp semi-skimmed milk

❊ Preheat the oven to 200 °C/400 °F/gas 6. Lightly grease and line the base of a 20-cm (8-in) round shallow cake tin with baking parchment. Trim and thinly slice the tomatoes, yellow pepper, courgette and salami, and arrange on the base of the tin.

❊ Sift the flours, baking powder and salt into a mixing bowl. Rub in the butter or margarine until the mixture resembles fine breadcrumbs, then stir in the cheese. In a separate bowl, lightly whisk the egg and milk together, then add to the dry ingredients and mix to a soft dough.

❊ On a lightly floured surface, roll out the dough to a circle just slightly smaller than the tin, then place it on top of the vegetables and salami. Bake for 20 minutes, or until well risen and golden-brown. Turn out onto a board and cut into wedges to serve.

Variation: *For a garlic mushroom pizza, gently cook 75 g (¾ cup) sliced button mushrooms in 1 tablespoon of light olive oil for 3–4 minutes until softened. Stir in 1 crushed garlic clove, then turn off the heat. Spoon into the base of the tin and spread out to an even layer, then top with the pastry, as before.*
Nutritional note: *We often think of pizzas as unhealthy fast food, but as long as you choose the topping carefully, they can make a well-balanced meal. Most children prefer yellow and red (bell) peppers as they are much sweeter than green ones. They also provide much more vitamin C, a boost to the immune system.*

These are especially good on a cold day and can be made with sweet potatoes for a change. If you're really short of time, cook the potatoes in the microwave until almost soft, then finish in the oven to brown and crisp the skin.

Simple jacket potatoes

SERVES 2

2 medium-sized baking potatoes

25 g (2 Tbsp) polyunsaturated margarine

2 rashers streaky bacon, de-rinded and chopped

4 spring onions (scallions), trimmed and finely sliced

2 Tbsp milk

50 g (2 oz) Gruyère or medium Cheddar, grated

Freshly ground black pepper, to taste

✳ Preheat the oven to 180 °C/350 °F/gas 4. Scrub and dry the potatoes, then prick with a fork and bake directly on the top oven shelf for 45 minutes, or until soft when gently squeezed. Leave for about 5 minutes, or until cool enough to handle.

✳ Meanwhile, melt the margarine in a small frying pan. When hot, add the bacon and fry until crisp. Remove with a slotted spoon, leaving the fat and juices behind. Transfer to a plate and set aside. Add the spring onions to the pan, lower the heat and cook for 2–3 minutes, stirring frequently until soft. Remove from the heat.

✳ Using a sharp knife, cut the baked potatoes in half lengthways, then scoop out the flesh, leaving a thin shell, and put the flesh in a bowl. Mash the potato with the milk until smooth, then add the bacon, spring onions and their juices and half the cheese. Season with pepper, if liked (you won't need salt as there's plenty in the bacon). Refill the jackets and sprinkle over the remaining cheese. Return to the oven and bake for 10 minutes, until the cheese is bubbling. Allow to cool for a few minutes before serving.

Tip: *To speed up oven cooking time, push a metal skewer through the middle of the potatoes during baking; this will help conduct heat to the centre.*
Nutritional note: *Potatoes are high in complex carbohydrates, so provide plenty of sustained energy. They also contain protein, fibre and small amounts of vitamins and minerals.*

This is a classic meal-in-a-bowl soup with tender chunks of chicken, juicy sweetcorn, celery and carrots. Nutritious noodles help to thicken the soup; break them into short lengths to make the soup easier to eat.

Chicken noodle soup

SERVES 4

600 ml (2½ cups) good-quality chicken stock

1 bay leaf

1 chicken breast, about 175 g (6 oz)

15 g (1 Tbsp) polyunsaturated margarine

1 onion, peeled and very finely chopped

1 stick of celery, finely chopped

1 carrot, peeled and finely chopped

75 g (2½ oz) fine egg noodles

200-g (7-oz) tin sweetcorn, drained

100 ml (scant ½ cup) semi-skimmed milk

1 Tbsp skimmed milk powder

Salt and freshly ground black pepper, to taste

✳ Pour the stock into a saucepan, add the bay leaf and bring to the boil. Add the chicken, then reduce the heat and simmer gently for about 12 minutes, until just cooked through. Remove the chicken with a slotted spoon and set aside to cool. Discard the bay leaf and pour the stock into a jug.

✳ Melt the margarine in the pan and gently cook the onion and celery for 7–8 minutes until softened. Add the carrot and stock and bring back to the boil. Simmer for 5 minutes, or until the vegetables are almost tender.

✳ Add the noodles to the soup and simmer for 2½ minutes. Meanwhile, cut the chicken into bite-sized pieces. Add the chicken and sweetcorn to the pan and simmer for a further minute, until the noodles are cooked. Stir in the milk, then sprinkle over the skimmed milk powder and stir briefly to dissolve. Add salt and pepper to taste, then ladle into bowls (use cold bowls for children to cool the soup a little). Serve straight away.

Tip: Left-over roast or shop-bought ready-cooked chicken can be used instead of a raw chicken breast in this recipe to save time.
Nutritional note: Adding skimmed milk powder not only gives soups a creamier taste, but increases the calcium content. It's a useful way of adding this mineral to your child's diet.

d these little pastries make

erve when their friends

ed mushrooms, (bell)

all work well.

ato squares

220 °C/425 °/gas 7. Remove

igerator about 15 minutes

start cooking, then carefully

ightly floured surface and cut

about 8 cm (3 in). Transfer them

, spacing the squares slightly

tres several times with a fork.

edges of each square, making

 in) wide.

and cut into 1-cm (½-in)

es in half. Put four tomato

top of each square, then

rella cubes. Bake the pastries

the pastry is well-risen and

nd bubbling. Cool for a few

Tip: *When brushing the edges with milk, take care not to dribble any down the cut sides of the pastry squares, or they won't rise as well.*
Nutritional note: *Mozzarella cheese is lower in fat than many other varieties of cheese. Like all dairy products, it is rich in calcium, needed by children and teenagers to maintain optimum bone and tooth development.*

Club sandwiches are an American invention and are a great way to serve two complementary fillings at the same time. Here, keeping the bacon separate from the creamy egg mayonnaise ensures it stays deliciously crisp.

Egg and bacon sandwich

SERVES 1

2 streaky bacon rashers, rinds removed

1 egg, hard-boiled, shelled and finely chopped

1 Tbsp mayonnaise

1 Tbsp Greek yoghurt

Salt and freshly ground black pepper, to taste

3 slices light rye or wholemeal bread, toasted and buttered

Shredded lettuce, watercress or cucumber slices

✣ Cook the bacon under a preheated hot grill for about 2 minutes on each side until lightly browned and crisp. Drain on kitchen paper and leave to cool. Meanwhile, mix the egg with the mayonnaise and yoghurt, seasoning with a little salt and pepper, if liked.

✣ Place one slice of toasted bread, butter-side up, on a board and arrange the bacon on top. Place a second slice of bread on top of the bacon, then add some shredded lettuce, watercress or cucumber slices. Spoon over the egg mayonnaise, then finish with the final slice of bread.

Tips: *Save time by buying ready-cooked bacon rashers; they're usually located in the cooked sliced meat section at the supermarket.*
✣ *Small mouths can't manage huge sandwiches, so slice the bread thinly and don't overdo the filling.*
Variations: *Smoked salmon and cream cheese: Sandwich two slices of bread with 25 g (1½ Tbsp) cream cheese, beaten until soft, with a few snipped fresh chives, if liked. Top with sliced smoked salmon and thinly sliced cucumber, then add the final slice of bread.*
✣ *Classic chicken and bacon club: Cut 50 g (2 oz) cooked chicken into bite-sized pieces and mix with the mayonnaise and yoghurt, instead of the egg.*

Traditionally, Spanish omelette is cooked on the hob and then the top is browned by placing it under a hot grill. Baking it in the oven is much simpler and you could make some garlic bread at the same time to accompany it.

Baked Spanish omelette

SERVES 4

2 Tbsp olive oil

1 small onion, peeled and sliced

2 medium-sized potatoes, about 300 g (10½ oz), peeled and cut into 1-cm (½-in) dice

½ red (bell) pepper, de-seeded and diced

1 garlic clove, peeled and crushed

75 g (½ cup) frozen peas, defrosted

4 eggs

125 ml (½ cup) semi-skimmed milk

Salt and freshly ground black pepper, to taste

✳ Preheat the oven to 180 °C/350 °F/gas 4. Grease the inside of a 20-cm (8-in) ovenproof dish with a teaspoon of the oil.

✳ Heat the remaining oil in a frying pan and gently cook the onion for 2 minutes. Add the potatoes, red pepper and garlic, and cook for a further 4–5 minutes, stirring occasionally, until the potatoes soften and begin to brown. Remove the pan from the heat, mix in the peas and tip into the prepared dish, evenly spreading out the mixture.

✳ Meanwhile, place the eggs with the milk and seasoning in a bowl and beat. Pour over the vegetables and bake in the oven for 30–40 minutes, or until lightly set. Remove from the oven, allow to stand for a few minutes, then loosen the edges with a palette knife and cut into wedges.

Variations: *Cheese and tomato: Leave out the red (bell) pepper and peas and arrange two thinly sliced tomatoes on top of the cooked vegetables. Sprinkle with 50 g (½ cup) grated Cheddar or Gruyère cheese before pouring over the eggs.*
✳ Sweetcorn: Use a drained 200-g (7-oz) tin of sweetcorn instead of the peas and red (bell) pepper, and instead of an ordinary onion, use a red one.

These can be served hot, but are also good cold for packed lunches and picnics. They freeze well, so are ideal for days when you know you'll be too busy to cook.

Mini meatballs

SERVES 4

For the meatballs

225 g (8 oz) extra lean minced beef

225 g (8 oz) sausage meat

1 Tbsp Worcestershire sauce

1 Tbsp tomato paste

Pinch of dried mixed herbs

1 Tbsp plain (all-purpose) flour

2 Tbsp sesame seeds

1 tsp olive oil

For the tomato dipping sauce

1 tsp olive oil

1 garlic clove, peeled and crushed

1 medium carrot, peeled and finely chopped

400-g (14-oz) tin chopped tomatoes

Pinch of caster (superfine) sugar

Salt and freshly ground black pepper

❊ Start by making the meatballs. Put the beef and sausage meat in a large bowl with the Worcestershire sauce, tomato paste and herbs. Mix together well, then using damp hands, shape the mixture into about 24 bite-sized balls. In a separate bowl, mix the flour and sesame seeds and roll the meatballs in the seed mixture, a few at a time, until coated all over. Chill until ready to cook.

❊ To make the sauce, heat the oil in a heavy-based saucepan and cook the garlic for a few seconds. Add the carrot, tomatoes and sugar and simmer uncovered for 15 minutes, or until the carrot is tender and the tomatoes well reduced. Transfer to a blender or food processor, add a little salt and pepper, and purée until smooth.

❊ Heat the oil for the meatballs in a large non-stick frying pan and sauté the meatballs in two or three batches (depending on the size of the pan) for 5–6 minutes, turning frequently until browned all over and cooked through (check this by cutting one of the meatballs in half). Lift out on to a plate lined with absorbent kitchen paper and keep warm. Serve hot with the dipping sauce and some salad or vegetable sticks.

Tip: *These little meatballs can be frozen after cooking. Open-freeze them on a tray, then pack in portions in freezer containers or bags.*
Nutritional note: *While most vegetables lose vitamins when cooked, tinned (and cooked fresh) tomatoes are the exception to this; cooking and canning them makes their nutrients more readily available.*

Burgers don't have to be made from beef. Here, bacon adds flavour and moistness to minced chicken and oats add a lovely texture. They're delicious with home-made or shop-bought sweetcorn relish.

Chicken and bacon burgers

SERVES 4

- 350 g (12½ oz) minced raw chicken
- 50 g (2 oz) streaky bacon, de-rinded and finely chopped
- 50 g (½ cup) porridge (rolled) oats
- 1 egg, lightly beaten
- ½ tsp dried mixed herbs
- Salt and freshly ground black pepper, to taste
- 1 Tbsp sunflower oil
- Wholemeal or white pitta breads, sliced tomatoes, lettuce and cucumber, to serve

❋ Put the chicken, bacon, oats, egg and herbs in a large bowl, adding salt and pepper to taste. Mix together until just combined (this is easiest done with your hands). Over-working the mixture will result in a tough burger, so don't overdo the mixing. Using wet hands, shape the mixture into 8 burgers, flattening them to about 2 cm (1 in) thick.

❋ Preheat the grill or a griddle pan to medium-hot. Brush the burgers with the oil. Grill for about 5 minutes, until browned, then turn over and cook for a further 5–6 minutes, lowering the heat for the last 2–3 minutes, to ensure the burgers are thoroughly cooked. Serve in warmed pitta breads with a few slices of tomato, lettuce and cucumber.

Tip: *Smaller children may prefer just one burger in a small pitta bread; those with larger appetites may cut a large pitta across into two pieces and serve a burger in each half.*

Nutritional note: *Chicken is rich in protein and contains all the essential amino acids needed for growth and cell repair. It is also a good source of the antioxidant selenium, which helps to protect against heart disease and some cancers.*

To freeze: *Uncooked burgers can be open-frozen then layered up with baking parchment before packing into a freezer container or bag.*

Also known as 'croque-monsieur' (croque meaning munch or crunch in French), this hot sandwich is a tasty treat that can be made in minutes and is perfect for a cold day. The sandwich may be fried in a little oil (see tip) or grilled, as here.

Cheese and ham toastie

SERVES 1

2 slices of medium-thickness white or wholemeal bread

15 g (1 Tbsp) polyunsaturated margarine

25 g (1 oz) Gruyère cheese, coarsely grated

1 slice of ham

❄ Thinly spread one side of each slice of bread with the butter or margarine. Sprinkle the cheese evenly over one of the buttered slices. Trim any visible fat from the ham, then lay on top of the cheese. Place the second slice of bread on top, butter-side down and gently press down to firm the sandwich. Trim off the crusts if liked with a serrated knife.

❄ Preheat the grill to medium-hot, then place the sandwich on the grill pan and cook for 2–3 minutes on each side until the bread is lightly browned and the cheese has melted. Allow the sandwich to cool for a minute (the cheese will be very hot), then cut into four triangles and serve. Some grilled halved tomatoes (grill at the same time as the sandwich) or some sticks of vegetable make a good accompaniment.

Tip: *If you decide to fry the sandwich, heat a good non-stick frying pan, add 2 teaspoons of sunflower oil and swirl over the base. Add the sandwich and cook for 2–3 minutes until the underside is browned and crisp, then turn over and cook for a further 2 minutes.*
Variation: *For the classic 'croque-madame', use sliced chicken instead of ham and top the sandwich with a poached or fried egg.*
Nutritional note: *Hard-cheeses such as Gruyère are a superb source of calcium, vital for growing healthy bones and strong teeth.*

Gently simmering pork spare ribs before roasting them ensures that they are really tender and also removes some of the fat. It also shortens the time needed to roast them in the oven.

Sticky finger ribs

SERVES 4

900 g (2 lb) meaty pork spare ribs, about 12 in total

2 Tbsp red wine vinegar

1 tsp sunflower oil

125 ml (½ cup) orange juice

1 Tbsp tomato paste

1 Tbsp light brown sugar

2 Tbsp Worcestershire sauce

2 tsp Dijon mustard

1 garlic clove, peeled and crushed

Salt and freshly ground black pepper, to taste

✱ Preheat the oven to 200 °C/400 °F/gas 6. Trim any excess fat from the ribs, then put them in a saucepan with just enough cold water to cover. Add 1 tablespoon of the vinegar and slowly bring to the boil. Skim the surface, then half-cover the pan with a lid and simmer for 15 minutes.

✱ Meanwhile, put all the remaining ingredients in to a small saucepan and bring to the boil, stirring occasionally. Simmer for 3–4 minutes until slightly reduced, then set aside. The sauce will thicken slightly as it starts to cool.

✱ Drain the ribs, discarding the water and place in a single layer in a roasting tin. Thickly brush with the sauce, turning to coat all over, then cover the top of the tin with foil and roast for 20 minutes. Remove the foil, turn the ribs and brush with any remaining sauce. Roast for a further 15–20 minutes, turning the ribs occasionally until well browned, sticky and tender. Allow the ribs to cool for a few minutes.

Tip: *Team these tasty ribs with some small baked potatoes cooked in the oven at the same time.*
Nutritional notes: *Roast the ribs until they are a rich mahogany colour, but do not let them char or burn, as this can produce chemicals linked with an increased risk of cancer.*

These make a change from sliced bread sandwiches and are great for packed lunches. Many children enjoy sweet and sour oriental sauces and condiments and here the tortilla is thinly spread with plum sauce, providing both flavour and moistness.

Chicken salad wrap

MAKES 1 WRAP

5-cm (2-in) piece of cucumber

75 g (2½ oz) cooked chicken breast, shredded

2 iceberg lettuce leaves (about 40 g/ 1½ oz), finely shredded

Salt and freshly ground black pepper, to taste

One 20-cm (8-in) wrap or flour tortilla

1 Tbsp plum or hoisin sauce

✳ Halve the cucumber lengthwise, scoop out the seeds, then cut into long, thin strips. Place in a bowl with the chicken and lettuce. Toss together, seasoning with a little salt and pepper, if liked.

✳ Place a large non-stick frying pan over a medium heat and heat the wrap for about 1 minute on each side, until just starting to turn golden. Remove from the pan and place on a board. Thinly spread the wrap with the plum sauce to within 1 cm (½ in) of the edges, then spoon the chicken mixture down the centre. Fold in the sides to enclose the filling and roll up tightly. Cut in half before serving.

Tip: *It isn't essential to cook the wrap, but it improves the flavour and it will be more supple and easier to fold.*

Variation: *For a Greek salad wrap, roughly dice a 5-cm (2-in) piece of cucumber and 1 large tomato (peel it first, if preferred). Mix with 25 g (1 oz) diced or crumbled feta cheese (soak in cold water for about 5 minutes before dicing to remove some of the salt). Brown the wrap as before, then spread with 1 heaped tablespoon of reduced-fat humous. Spoon the filling down the centre, add a few chopped stoned olives if liked, then roll up as before.*

Nutritional note: *On the glycaemic index (the time a food takes to raise blood sugar) tortillas have approximately half the rating of that of wholemeal bread, so provide a steadier, more sustained rise in blood sugar levels, helping to keep children's energy levels constant.*

meat & fish

Stir-fries are healthy and quick to cook. While many children don't like the chewy texture of meat, they'll happily eat it if it is cut into wafer-thin slices. Here, marinating helps to tenderise the meat as well as enhancing its flavour.

Sizzling beef stir-fry

SERVES 4

300 g (10½ oz) sirloin or rump steak

2 tsp sesame oil

2 Tbsp soy sauce

2 Tbsp medium sherry*

2.5-cm (1-in) piece of root ginger, grated

2 medium carrots, peeled

4 spring onions (scallions)

150 g (5½ oz) mange-touts (snow peas)

150 g (5½ oz) baby sweetcorn

200 g (7 oz) fine egg noodles

1 Tbsp groundnut or sunflower oil

½ tsp cornflour

5 Tbsp concentrated beef or vegetable stock

** During cooking all the alcohol from the sherry will evaporate, just leaving the flavour behind, but if you prefer, use orange juice instead.*

❊ Trim any excess fat from the steak, then cut into thin strips across the grain. Put the beef strips into a bowl with 1 teaspoon of the sesame oil, the soy sauce and sherry. Squeeze the juices from the root ginger over the beef, then stir well. Set aside for at least 10 minutes, or if time allows, for up to 2 hours in the refrigerator.

❊ Cut the carrots into thin matchstick strips about 5 cm (2 in) long. Cut the spring onions across in half, then into shreds lengthways. Halve the mange-touts and baby sweetcorn lengthways. Bring a large pan of water to the boil. Add the egg noodles and stir, then cover the pan, lower the heat and simmer for 3 minutes, or according to the packet instructions, until the noodles are barely tender. Drain well.

❊ Meanwhile, heat a wok or a large deep non-stick frying pan until hot. Add the remaining sesame oil and groundnut or sunflower oil and swirl it around to coat the base of the pan. Add the beef, reserving the marinade, and stir-fry over a high heat for 2 minutes, until lightly browned. Remove from the wok and set aside. Stir-fry the carrots for a minute, then add the spring onions, mange-touts and sweetcorn. Stir-fry for a further minute. Blend the cornflour with the reserved marinade and stock. Add to the pan with the beef and noodles and let the mixture bubble for a few seconds. Add the noodles and cook for a further minute, or until everything is piping hot. Serve straight away.

Variation: *Pork tenderloin makes an excellent alternative to beef in this dish. Nutritional note: Stir-frying is a healthy way to cook as the meat is very lean and only a little oil is needed. Cooking quickly over a high heat ensures that the maximum amount of vitamins in the vegetables is retained.*

Making individual portions is useful when you want to freeze some for later use. These pies have a golden vegetable topping and contain lentils which help to enrich and thicken the meat mixture, but virtually disappear as they cook.

Beef and potato pies

MAKES 4 PORTIONS

For the meat mixture

1 Tbsp sunflower oil

1 onion, peeled and finely chopped

1 stick celery, finely chopped

1 garlic clove, peeled and crushed

400 g (14 oz) lean minced beef

2 Tbsp red lentils

400-g (14-oz) tin chopped tomatoes

250 ml (1 cup) beef stock

1 tsp dried mixed herbs

125 g (1 cup) frozen peas, defrosted

Salt and freshly ground black pepper, to taste

For the topping

675 g (1 lb 11 oz) potatoes, peeled and cut into chunks

225 g (8 oz) carrots, peeled and sliced

50 g (2 oz) Cheddar cheese, grated

2 Tbsp semi-skimmed milk

Salt and freshly ground black pepper, to taste

Tip: *This is a good opportunity to introduce new vegetables to your children: diced swede (rutabaga), mushrooms and (bell) peppers all work well. If you're planning to freeze any portions, do this before oven-cooking. Defrost in the refrigerator overnight, then cook as before.*

Nutritional note: *High in iron, lentils may help protect against anaemia and tiredness and are virtually fat-free.*

⁂ Start by making the meat mixture. Heat the oil in a large saucepan and gently cook the onion for 3 minutes. Add the celery and garlic and cook for a further 3–4 minutes, until almost soft. Stir in the beef and cook, stirring, over a high heat until browned. Stir in the lentils, tomatoes, stock, herbs and seasoning. Bring to the boil, half-cover the pan with a lid and simmer for 40 minutes, or until the meat is tender and the sauce is well reduced. Check the seasoning, then divide the mixture between four 300-ml (1¼-cup) individual ovenproof dishes.

⁂ To make the topping, cook the potatoes and carrots in lightly salted boiling water for about 15 minutes, or until tender. Drain thoroughly, then mash with the cheese and milk, salt and pepper. Using a wooden spoon, beat until fluffy.

⁂ Place a baking tray in the oven, then preheat to 200 °C/400 °F/gas 6. Spoon and spread the potato and carrot over the meat mixture. Place the individual dishes on the preheated baking tray and bake for 25–30 minutes, or until the meat mixture is hot and bubbling and the topping is browned. Allow the pies to cool for a few minutes before serving.

Popular with the whole family, this meal is delicious served with a simple tomato sauce and baked potatoes cooked in the oven at the same time. Any leftovers can be served cold and are great for picnics and packed lunches.

Meatloaf

SERVES 4–6

For the meatloaf

2 slices medium-thickness white or wholemeal bread

2 Tbsp milk

1 egg, lightly beaten

225 g (8 oz) lean minced beef

225 g (8 oz) minced pork or good quality pork sausage meat

1 small onion, peeled and very finely chopped

2 garlic cloves, peeled and very finely chopped

1 tsp chopped fresh thyme or dried mixed herbs

1 Tbsp sun-dried tomato paste

Salt and freshly ground black pepper, to taste

For the tomato sauce

1 Tbsp olive oil

1 small onion, peeled and finely chopped

1 garlic clove, peeled and finely chopped

400-g (14-oz) tin chopped tomatoes

1 Tbsp sun-dried tomato paste

Tip: *If you are planning to serve the meatloaf cold, allow it to cool in the tin before turning out. Wrap in greaseproof paper and foil and chill until ready to serve. This tomato sauce is also delicious served with pasta, so it's worth making double the quantity. It may be stored for up to 3 days in the refrigerator, or frozen for up to 2 months.*
Nutritional note: *Garlic is a versatile ingredient and can add a subtle hint of flavour. It contains allicin which helps strengthen the immune system.*

* Preheat the oven to 190 °C/375 °F/ gas 5. Grease a 450-g (1-lb) loaf tin and line the base with baking parchment. Tear the bread into small pieces and put in a large bowl. Drizzle over the milk and beaten egg and leave to soak for 5 minutes, then mash into smaller pieces with a fork. Add the beef, pork or sausage meat, onion, garlic, herbs and tomato paste to the soaked bread. Mix all the ingredients together thoroughly, seasoning well with salt and pepper. Spoon the mixture into the loaf tin and level the top. Bake in the centre of the oven for 1 hour.

* Meanwhile, make the sauce. Heat the oil in a saucepan, add the onion and cook gently for about 10 minutes until softened. Stir in the garlic and cook for a further minute, stirring, then add the tomatoes and tomato paste. Cook uncovered over a low heat for 15–20 minutes, stirring occasionally, until the sauce is thick. Leave to cool for a few minutes, then purée the sauce in a food processor or blender until smooth. Pour back into the pan, season to taste and reheat until bubbling. Allow the meatloaf to stand for 10 minutes, then loosen the sides with a knife and turn it out carefully. Cut into thick slices and serve with the sauce and baked potatoes, green beans and carrots.

Food on skewers always seems to taste so much nicer! But for very young children, remove the meat from the skewers before serving.

Lamb skewers with golden rice

SERVES 4

For the skewers

450 g (1 lb) lean minced lamb

½ small onion, peeled and grated

½ tsp ground paprika

¼ tsp ground cinnamon

Salt and freshly ground black pepper, to taste

2 Tbsp plain (all-purpose) flour, for dusting

For the golden rice

1 Tbsp olive oil

½ small onion, peeled and finely chopped

350 g (1¾ cups) long grain rice

1 bay leaf

2 whole cloves

¼ tsp ground turmeric

900 ml (3¾ cups) vegetable stock

175 g (1 cup) frozen peas, defrosted

✽ Start by preparing the skewers. Put the minced lamb, grated onion, paprika and cinnamon in a bowl. Season with salt and pepper, then mix well. With flour-dusted hands, shape the mixture into 16 egg-shaped balls and thread them onto four oiled metal kebab skewers.

✽ For the rice, heat the oil in a large saucepan and gently cook the onion for 8–10 minutes, until softened. Add the rice to the pan and stir to coat the grains in the oil, then add the bay leaf, cloves and turmeric. Pour over the stock and bring to the boil. Cover and cook for 10–12 minutes, or until the rice is tender and the stock absorbed, stirring in the peas 3 minutes before the end of cooking time.

✽ Meanwhile, preheat the grill to moderately hot and cook the kebabs for about 10 minutes, turning occasionally until well browned on all sides. Serve with the golden rice, removing the lamb meatballs from the skewers when serving to younger children. If liked, make a minty yoghurt dipping sauce by stirring 2 teaspoons of mint sauce into 150 ml (⅔ cup) thick natural or Greek yoghurt.

Variation: *These are also delicious made with lean minced beef instead of lamb, and parsley instead of mint. If liked, grill a few halved tomatoes alongside the kebabs.*

Nutritional note: *Unlike some meats, lamb is naturally rather than intensively reared. It is particularly rich in niacin (B3), which is required for the release of energy from food and also zinc, vital for teenage boys.*

Although often made with minced beef, this well-known Tex-Mex dish was originally made with finely chopped beef. Serve with baked potatoes or rice to balance the meal.

Chilli con carne

SERVES 4

For the chilli

350 g (12½ oz) lean braising steak

1 tsp plain (all-purpose) flour

1½ Tbsp sunflower oil

1 small onion, peeled and finely chopped

1 garlic clove, peeled and finely chopped

2 tsp mild chilli powder

1 tsp ground cumin

1 medium carrot, peeled and coarsely grated

300 ml (1¼ cups) beef stock

200-g (7-oz) tin chopped tomatoes

1 Tbsp tomato paste

½ tsp dried mixed herbs

Salt and freshly ground black pepper, to taste

200-g (7-oz) tin red kidney beans, rinsed and drained

½ tsp dark brown sugar

For the topping (optional)

150 ml (⅔ cup) soured cream, half-fat crème fraîche, or Greek yoghurt

2 Tbsp snipped chives

Nutritional note: *Including red kidney beans in this dish allows the quantity of meat to be reduced while keeping a good protein and iron content. Kidney beans are also high in dietary fibre, which is important for digestive health.*
Variations: *Chilli con carne is delicious spooned into soft tortillas (allow two per person) and sprinkled with some grated mature Cheddar or Manchego cheese.*
✻ For a herby potato topping, simmer a combination of ordinary and sweet potatoes, about 675 g (1 lb 8 oz) peeled and cut into chunks, for 15 minutes, or until tender. Drain well and mash with 25 g (2 Tbsp) polyunsaturated margarine, 3 tablespoons of milk, and some seasoning. Beat in 2 tablespoons of chopped fresh herbs, such as chives or parsley. Spoon the chilli into an ovenproof dish, spread the potato mixture on top and bake at 180 °C/350 °F/gas 4 for 25 minutes.

✳ To make the chilli, cut the meat into 1-cm (½-in) thin strips, then cut it crossways into small cubes. Sprinkle the flour over the meat to coat. Heat 2 teaspoons of the oil in a large flameproof casserole or heavy-based saucepan. Add the meat and cook over a moderately high heat until browned on all sides. Remove from the pan and set aside. Heat the remaining oil in the pan, add the onion and gently cook for 10 minutes, until very soft. Add the garlic, chilli powder, cumin and carrot and cook for a further minute, stirring frequently.

✳ Return the meat to the pan, then stir in the stock, chopped tomatoes, tomato paste, herbs and a little salt and pepper. Bring to the boil, reduce the heat to a gentle simmer, cover and cook for 30 minutes. Stir in the kidney beans and simmer, uncovered, for a further 15 minutes, stirring occasionally, until the meat is very tender and the sauce well-reduced.

✳ For the topping, stir together the soured cream, crème fraîche or yoghurt with the chives. Spoon the chilli con carne onto warmed plates, topped with a large spoonful of the cream and chive mixture and serve with baked potatoes or rice.

Pork and pineapple make perfect partners and here they are cooked with colourful vegetables in a simple mouthwatering Chinese-style sauce.

Sweet and sour pork

SERVES 4

- 350 g (12½ oz) pork fillet
- 2 tsp groundnut or sunflower oil
- 2 tsp cornflour
- 1 Tbsp clear honey
- 1 Tbsp soy sauce
- 1 Tbsp sherry vinegar
- 150 ml (⅔ cup) vegetable stock
- 2.5-cm (1-in) piece fresh root ginger, grated
- 225-g (8-oz) tin pineapple chunks in natural juice
- 1 small red (bell) pepper, de-seeded and sliced
- 125 g (4½ oz) baby sweetcorn, halved
- Steamed or boiled rice or noodles, to serve

❋ Trim any visible fat from the pork and cut into 1-cm (½-in) thick slices. Heat the oil in a non-stick frying pan, then fry the meat for about 2 minutes on each side, or until lightly browned. Remove from the pan and set aside.

❋ Blend the cornflour, honey, soy sauce and vinegar together in a jug. Stir in the stock and the squeezed juices from the ginger. Drain the juice from the pineapple, reserving the chunks and stir this in as well. Pour into the pan and bring to the boil, stirring until thickened. Add the red pepper and sweetcorn and simmer uncovered for 2 minutes. Return the pork to the pan with the pineapple chunks and simmer for a further 3–4 minutes, or until the meat and vegetables are tender.

Tip: *Vary the vegetable content if you like: halved mange-touts (snow peas) or green beans, sliced mushrooms and shredded pak choi all work well.*
Nutritional note: *Lean pork such as fillet has a fat content of only 3 per cent, much the same as that contained in skinless chicken breast, and lower than lamb or beef.*

Baking fish in baking parchment is a healthy way to keep it moist and succulent and retains all the vitamins. It's also great fun to eat!

Fish and vegetable parcels

SERVES 4

4 pieces of white fish, such as cod or salmon fillets, each weighing about 125 g (4½ oz)

4 tsp fresh lemon juice

Salt and freshly ground black pepper, to taste

2 carrots, peeled and cut into matchstick strips

1 celery stick, cut into matchstick strips

1 leek, thinly sliced

150 g (5½ oz) baby button mushrooms, halved

4 small sprigs of fresh parsley

✳ Preheat the oven to 180 °C/350 °F/gas 4. Cut out four 20 cm (8 in) circles from baking parchment. Place a piece of fish on one half of each circle and sprinkle with 1 teaspoon of lemon juice, then lightly season with salt and pepper. Scatter over the carrots, celery, leek and baby mushrooms and add a parsley sprig to each.

✳ Fold over the top half of the circle, then close the parcels by turning and pleating the edges of the paper. Place on a baking tray and bake for 15 minutes. Remove from the oven and leave to stand for a minute or two, then transfer the parcels to warmed plates and serve with some new potatoes or steamed rice.

Tip: *Snip a small hole in the top of each parcel to allow some of the hot steam to escape before serving.*
Nutritional note: *White fish is a great high-protein, low-fat food and providing any skin and bones are removed, is easy to eat. White sea fish are particularly valuable in the diet for their high iodine content, important for the production of hormones.*

These fishcakes can be prepared from freshly cooked or leftover mashed potato. Because they already contain potatoes and sweetcorn, a few steamed green beans, peas or crunchy coleslaw is the only accompaniment needed.

Tempting tuna fishcakes

SERVES 4

675 g (1 lb 8 oz) floury potatoes, such as King Edward or Maris Piper, peeled

25 g (2 Tbsp) polyunsaturated margarine

1 Tbsp mayonnaise

2 Tbsp chopped parsley

Salt and freshly ground black pepper

185-g (6½-oz) tin tuna chunks, drained

200-g (7-oz) tin sweetcorn, drained

2 Tbsp plain (all-purpose) flour, for coating

1 Tbsp sunflower oil, for shallow frying

✱ Cut the potatoes into even-sized chunks and place in a saucepan. Pour in enough boiling water to just cover them and cook gently for 15 minutes, or until tender. Drain thoroughly and return to the pan with the margarine and mash until very smooth. Beat in the mayonnaise and parsley and season to taste with salt and pepper. Gently stir in the tuna and sweetcorn.

✱ Shape the mixture into eight thick flat round cakes, each measuring about 8 cm (3 in) in diameter. Lightly dust them with the flour. Heat half the oil in a non-stick frying pan and cook four of the fishcakes for 3–4 minutes on each side until golden-brown. Remove from the pan with a fish slice and keep warm while cooking the remaining fishcakes in the rest of the oil. Serve hot with some freshly cooked vegetables, salad or coleslaw.

Nutritional note: *Oily fish such as tuna is an excellent source of omega 3, needed for healthy brain growth and development. A high intake may increase the ability to concentrate, particularly in children who have a history of attention deficit disorder and hyperactivity.*

Make ahead: *These fishcakes can be made up to 24 hours before cooking. Place on baking parchment and chill in the refrigerator, covered with clingfilm, until needed.*

Unlike commercial varieties, these chicken dippers are made with lean chicken breast and avoid deep-frying, so are high in protein and low in fat. They're delicious served with potato wedges (see page 92).

Crunchy chicken dippers

SERVES 4

3 boneless, skinless chicken breasts, about 150 g (5½ oz) each

50 g (½ cup) wholemeal flour

25 g (1 oz) Cheddar cheese, finely grated

1 Tbsp sesame seeds

Salt and freshly ground black pepper

1 egg white

2 Tbsp cold water

✳ Preheat the oven to 200 °C/400 °F/gas 6. Cut the chicken breasts into strips about 4 cm (1½ in) long. Mix the flour, cheese, sesame seeds and a little salt and pepper together on a plate. Put the egg white and water in a shallow bowl and lightly whisk together with a fork. Dip the chicken strips in the egg white, then roll in the flour and cheese mixture until well coated. Transfer to a lightly greased non-stick baking tray.

✳ Bake the dippers on the top shelf of the oven for 12 minutes, turning once, or until the chicken is cooked through. Transfer to serving plates and allow to cool for a minute or two before serving with creamed potatoes or potato wedges, baked beans or peas.

Tips: *Save the egg yolk and use in another recipe, such as Vanilla ice cream (see page 132).*

✳ *Make a quick and healthy dip by stirring a 5-cm (2-in) piece finely diced cucumber and a small grated carrot into 2 tablespoons of mayonnaise mixed with 1 tablespoon of tomato ketchup.*

Nutritional note: *Although only a small amount is used in this recipe, sesame seeds are rich in the minerals iron, calcium, zinc and selenium. However, a very small number of children have an allergy to these.*

Made with a tomato- and herb-flavoured batter that can be quickly whisked together by hand, these mini versions of toad in the hole make a simple yet nutritious and filling meal.

Sausage and tomato popovers

SERVES 4

150 g (1½ cups) plain (all-purpose) flour

25 g (¼ cup) wholemeal flour

½ tsp salt

3 eggs

2 tsp sun-dried tomato paste

1 tsp dried mixed herbs

350 ml (1½ cups) milk

1 Tbsp sunflower oil

24 cocktail sausages

✽ Sift the flours and salt into a mixing bowl, adding any bran left in the sieve and make a well in the middle. Break the eggs into the well, add the tomato paste, herbs and milk, and gradually work the flour into the liquid to make a smooth thin batter. Pour into a large jug and set aside.

✽ Preheat the oven to 220 °C/425 °F/gas 7. Using a piece of kitchen paper and the oil, lightly grease a 12-hole deep non-stick muffin tin. Each hole should measure 6 cm (2½ in) across the top. Prick the sausages with a fork, then place 2 sausages side by side in each hole. Cook in the oven for 4 minutes, until the sausages are beginning to brown and sizzle.

✽ Remove from the oven and quickly divide the batter evenly among the muffin cups; it should come three quarters of the way up each hole. Bake for about 10 minutes, then reduce the oven temperature to 200 °C/400 °F/gas 6 and cook for a further 25 minutes, until the popovers are golden-brown, well-risen and crisp. Serve hot with baked beans.

Variation: *For a vegetarian version, replace the cocktail sausages with sliced vegetarian sausages (pre-cook these for 2 minutes only) or add some chopped vegetables such as courgettes (zucchini) and (bell) peppers.*
Nutritional note: *Many sausages contain poor quality meat, cheap fillers and additives. Buy from a good butcher, or use 'premium' chipolata sausages and squeeze and twist each into smaller cocktail-sized sausages, or simply cut in half.*

This impressive-looking dish is surprisingly simple to make. Chicken breasts are rolled up with Gruyère and lean ham before cooking, to give a 'Swiss roll' appearance when sliced.

Chicken roulade

SERVES 4

- 4 boneless, skinless chicken breasts
- 4 thin slices Gruyère cheese
- 4 slices lean ham
- Salt and freshly ground black pepper
- 1 Tbsp sunflower oil
- 1 garlic clove, peeled
- 1 bay leaf
- 150 ml (⅔ cup) well-flavoured chicken stock
- ½ tsp cornflour
- 2 Tbsp Greek yoghurt
- 1 Tbsp chopped fresh herbs, such as parsley or chives (optional)

⁂ On a board, slice a chicken breast horizontally about three-quarters of the way through, then open up. Cover with a piece of lightly oiled baking parchment, then flatten by gently bashing with a rolling pin. Repeat with the remaining breasts. Top each with a slice of Gruyère, then a slice of ham. Season with salt and pepper, roll up and secure with wooden cocktail sticks.

⁂ Heat the oil in an ovenproof casserole and fry the chicken for 2–3 minutes on each side until lightly browned. Add the garlic clove and bay leaf to the casserole, then pour in the chicken stock. Cover with the lid and simmer gently for 15–20 minutes, turning once, or until the chicken is cooked through. Remove the chicken from the casserole dish, cover with foil and leave to 'rest' for 5 minutes (this makes it easier to slice).

⁂ Strain the stock and juices from the chicken into a small pan and bring to a rapid boil. Boil for 3–4 minutes until well-reduced, then reduce the heat to a gentle simmer. Blend the cornflour and yoghurt together and stir into the stock. Simmer for 1 minute, stirring until thickened, then stir in the herbs, if liked.

⁂ Slice the chicken and arrange on warmed serving plates. Spoon over the sauce. Serve with new or creamed potatoes or rice and some steamed vegetables such as carrots and peas.

This simple dish is a great introduction to curries. Coconut milk, thick yoghurt and subtle spices add an aromatic note. Serve with plain steamed or boiled rice and peas.

Creamy chicken korma

SERVES 4

4 skinless boneless chicken breasts

1 Tbsp sunflower oil

1 onion, peeled and finely chopped

2 garlic cloves, peeled and crushed

1 tsp ground cumin

2 tsp ground coriander

½ tsp ground ginger

½ tsp ground turmeric

2 tsp cornflour

300 ml (1¼ cups) thick plain yoghurt

150 ml (⅔ cup) reduced-fat coconut milk

100 ml (scant ½ cup) chicken stock

Pinch of salt

2 Tbsp chopped fresh coriander (cilantro) (optional)

✳ Cut each chicken breast into three or four pieces and set aside. Heat the oil in a large saucepan and gently cook the onion for 10 minutes, until very soft. Add the garlic and spices and cook for a further minute, stirring all the time.

✳ Blend the cornflour with a large spoonful of yoghurt, then stir this mixture into the rest of the yoghurt. Stir into the spicy mixture, a spoonful at a time, then gradually stir in the coconut milk and stock. Add the chicken, then bring the mixture to a very gentle simmer, stirring frequently until thickened. Cover and simmer for 20 minutes, or until the chicken is thoroughly cooked, stirring occasionally. Season with a little salt, then stir in the fresh coriander, if using. Serve with plain steamed or boiled rice, peas or a side salad such as chopped cucumber and tomatoes.

Tip: *To spice up this dish for adults, serve with some hot-spiced poppadoms or naan breads.* **Nutritional note:** *Most of the fat in chicken is in the skin, so providing this is removed, it is one of the lowest-fat meats.*

Beefburgers needn't be unhealthy if you use good-quality lean minced beef. These are flavoured with soy sauce and herbs, and have a melting mozzarella centre. Serve in wholemeal burger buns with potato wedges and a salad.

Cheesy beefburgers with potato wedges

SERVES 4

For the burgers

450 g (1 lb) lean minced beef

1 Tbsp soy or Worcestershire sauce

1 tsp dried mixed herbs

Salt and freshly ground black pepper, to taste

50 g (2 oz) mozzarella or Cheddar cheese

For the potato wedges

675 g (1 lb 8 oz) medium-sized potatoes, scrubbed

600 ml (2½ cups) boiling vegetable stock

1 Tbsp sunflower oil

❉ Preheat the oven to 200 °C/400 °F/gas 6. Put the minced beef, soy or Worcestershire sauce and mixed herbs in a large bowl. Season with salt and pepper and mix together well. Divide the mixture into four equal portions and shape each piece into a large flat round. Cut the cheese into four pieces, then place a piece in the centre of each beef round. Gently mould the beef around the cheese, shaping into a burger slightly thicker than 1 cm (½ in). Arrange on a non-stick baking tray.

❉ Put a second non-stick baking tray in the oven to heat. Cut the potatoes in half lengthways, then cut each half into thick wedges. Place in a large saucepan, pour over the stock and bring back to the boil. Cover and simmer for 3 minutes, or until almost tender. Drain well. Put the wedges in a large bowl, drizzle over the oil and toss until lightly coated. Tip onto the preheated baking tray and bake on the top shelf of the oven.

❉ When the potato wedges have been cooking for 10 minutes, put the burgers in the oven on the shelf below the potato wedges. Cook for 20 minutes, turning them and the potato wedges over halfway through cooking.

Tender chunks of chicken and juicy mushrooms are cooked in a smooth all-in-one white sauce beneath a crisp filo pastry topping.

Chicken and mushroom pie

SERVES 4

For the filling

25 g (2 Tbsp) polyunsaturated margarine

125 g (4½ oz) whole baby button mushrooms

40 g (¼ cup) plain (all-purpose) flour

600 ml (2½ cups) semi-skimmed milk

¼ chicken stock cube

Pinch of mixed dried herbs

3 skinless, boneless chicken breasts, cut into 2.5-cm (1-in) cubes

Salt and freshly ground black pepper, to taste

For the topping

5 sheets of filo pastry (75 g / 2½ oz)

25 g (2 Tbsp) polyunsaturated margarine, melted

✤ Preheat the oven to 190 °C/375 °F/gas 5. Melt the margarine in a saucepan and gently cook the mushrooms for 4–5 minutes, or until lightly browned and almost tender. Using a slotted spoon, transfer the mushrooms to a small bowl, leaving the juices behind. Stir the flour into the juices and add a little milk to make a smooth paste, then gradually stir in the remaining milk. Add the stock cube and herbs and bring to the boil, stirring until thickened.

✤ Add the chicken to the sauce and bring back to the boil. Gently simmer for 3 minutes, then season with salt and pepper. Spoon the mixture into a 1.5-litre (6-cup) oven-proof pie or baking dish.

✤ Brush a sheet of filo pastry with a little of the melted margarine, then crumple it up loosely and place, margarine-side up, over the filling. Repeat with the remaining pastry and melted margarine. Bake in the oven for 25 minutes, or until the pastry is golden brown and crisp. Serve with creamed potatoes and green beans or peas.

Tip: *If preferred, a tablespoon of olive oil may be used instead of the melted margarine for brushing the pastry.*
Nutritional note: *Filo is a healthy low-fat pastry and only a little is needed to make this crispy pie topping. Filo is made mainly from wheat flour, water and a small amount of vegetable oil, so is suitable for vegans.*

Children enjoy food on skewers, but even the most careful child should be supervised. When feeding younger children, remove the meat from the skewers before serving.

Teriyaki turkey with carrot and courgette noodles

SERVES 4

- 350 g (12½ oz) turkey breast
- 2 Tbsp Japanese soy sauce
- 2 Tbsp orange juice
- 1 garlic clove, peeled and crushed
- 1 tsp caster (superfine) sugar
- 2.5-cm (1-in) piece fresh ginger, peeled and grated
- 300 g (10½ oz) medium egg noodles
- 2 carrots, peeled and cut into matchstick strips
- 1 courgette (zucchini), trimmed, halved lengthways and thinly sliced
- 1 Tbsp sesame seeds

✻ Cut the turkey into strips. Put the soy sauce, orange juice, garlic, sugar and ginger in a bowl and whisk together with a fork. Add the turkey and stir to coat. Cover and marinate in the refrigerator for 30 minutes.

✻ Meanwhile, lightly oil eight metal skewers or soak bamboo skewers in cold water (this helps prevent them burning). Preheat the grill to medium-high. Thread the marinated turkey strips onto the skewers, reserving the marinade. Cook the skewers under the grill for about 5 minutes, turning them frequently and basting with the marinade for the first 3 minutes (don't baste for the last couple of minutes as the marinade contains raw turkey juices). Sprinkle the skewers with sesame seeds and grill for a few more seconds until the seeds are golden.

✻ While the turkey is cooking, cook the noodles in boiling water or stock following the packet instructions. Add the carrots and courgette for the last 3 minutes. Drain well and divide between warmed plates. Top each with two turkey skewers and serve immediately.

Variation: *Chicken makes a good alternative to turkey breast. If liked, add extra vegetables such as baby button mushrooms to the skewers.*
Nutritional note: *Turkey is a good source of zinc, vital for growth, as well s for the efficient functioning of the immune system. It is particularly important for boys as they approach their teenage years and during adolescence, so encourage them to enjoy this meat from an early age.*

Chicken cooked on the bone can be really flavoursome and tender, yet chicken thighs are often overlooked. Here, they are skinned and the meat slashed to allow the sauce to flavour and tenderise the meat. Accompany with Boston-style baked beans for a truly tasty meal.

Maple-glazed chicken and Boston beans

SERVES 4

For the chicken

- 25 g (2 Tbsp) butter or polyunsaturated margarine
- 4 Tbsp maple syrup
- 1 tsp Dijon mustard
- 8 chicken thighs, skins removed
- Salt and freshly ground black pepper

For the Boston beans

- 1 tsp olive oil
- 125 g (4½ oz) smoked streaky bacon, diced
- 1 small onion, peeled and very finely chopped
- 400-g (14-oz) tin cannellini or borlotti beans, drained and rinsed
- 150 ml (⅔ cup) passata (strained tomatoes)
- 2 tsp molasses or black treacle
- 2 tsp Worcestershire sauce

Tips: *Measure the molasses or black treacle by dipping the measuring spoon into near-boiling water first.*
❄ *Passata is a smooth purée of tomatoes, sold in bottles. You can make your own by blending tinned tomatoes in a food processor until smooth, then sieving to remove any tomato seeds.*
Nutritional note: *Although only used in small quantities in this recipe, molasses is rich in many minerals, including iron, calcium, magnesium, copper, phosphorus, potassium and zinc. All these are needed to maintain a healthy body.*

✳ Preheat the oven to 180 °C/350 °F/
gas 4. Start by preparing the chicken.
Put the butter or margarine, maple syrup
and mustard in a small saucepan and
gently heat until just melted. Stir the
mixture together, remove from the heat
and leave to cool. Make two or three
shallow slashes on the flesh of each
chicken thigh, then place in an
ovenproof dish, spacing them slightly
apart. Season with a little salt and
pepper if liked, then thickly brush over
the maple syrup mixture. Bake in the
oven for 30 minutes, then baste the
chicken and cook for a further 10–15
minutes, or until the chicken is dark
golden and tender.

✳ Meanwhile, make the beans.
Heat the oil in a large saucepan and
cook the bacon over a high heat until
lightly browned and crisp. Remove from
the pan with a slotted spoon and set
aside. Drain off the excess fat from the
pan, leaving just 1 teaspoon behind.
Add the onion to the pan and gently
cook for about 10 minutes until soft.
Stir in the beans, passata, molasses
and Worcestershire sauce. Cover and
simmer for 5 minutes, then stir in the
crispy bacon. Spoon the beans onto
serving plates and serve with the
chicken.

This is a great way to introduce your children to fresh salmon. These fingers have a crisp crumb coating which helps to keep the fish moist and juicy.

Salmon fish fingers with pea and potato mash

SERVES 4

450-g (1-lb) piece fresh salmon fillet, skinned

3 Tbsp plain (all-purpose) flour

Salt and freshly ground black pepper, to taste

1 egg, lightly beaten

75 g (¾ cup) dry white breadcrumbs

2 tsp finely grated lemon zest (optional)

675 g (1⅓ cups) floury potatoes, peeled and cut into large chunks

200 g (7 oz) frozen peas, defrosted

2 Tbsp semi-skimmed milk

25 g (2 Tbsp) sunflower margarine

1 Tbsp olive oil

❊ Pat the fish fillet dry with absorbent kitchen paper, then place on a board and cut into eight fingers, each about 10 x 2.5 cm (4 x 1 in). Lightly season the flour with salt and pepper in a shallow bowl, lightly beat the egg in another bowl, and mix together the breadcrumbs and lemon zest in a third. Dip each piece of salmon first in the flour, shaking off the excess, then into the beaten egg and finally in the breadcrumbs. Place on a plate and chill until ready to cook.

❊ Cook the potatoes in a large saucepan of lightly boiling water for 15 minutes, adding the peas for the last 2 minutes of cooking time. Drain thoroughly, then return to the pan with the milk and margarine and mash until smooth. Beat with a wooden spoon for a minute or two until fluffy.

❊ While the potatoes and peas are cooking, heat the oil in a non-stick frying pan until hot. Add the salmon fingers, reduce the heat to medium and gently cook for 10 minutes, turning once until the outsides are golden brown and the salmon is just cooked. Serve straight away with the pea and potato mash. Adults may enjoy a wedge of lemon to squeeze over the salmon.

Tip: *Make the breadcrumbs from bread a day or two old in a food processor, working them until very fine, then spread out on a tray and leave them to dry for a few hours, or overnight, if preferred.*

Make ahead: *The salmon fingers may be prepared 12 hours ahead of cooking. Place them on a sheet of baking parchment on a plate (otherwise they will stick) and cover tightly with clingfilm. Keep in the refrigerator until ready to cook.*

Nutritional note: *Like all oily fish, salmon is a good source of omega 3 fats, best known for their beneficial effects on the heart, but which are also important for brain function and may improve concentration.*

This dish is a tasty combination of haddock and prawns in a smooth sauce topped with a layer of grated vegetables. It is a complete meal by itself, although you may like to serve it with some peas or sweetcorn as well.

Rosti-topped fish pie

SERVES 4

For the fish mixture

40 g (3 Tbsp) butter or polyunsaturated margarine

50 g (½ cup) plain (all-purpose) flour

150 ml (⅔ cup) fish or vegetable stock

450 ml (1¾ cups) semi-skimmed milk

1 Tbsp lemon juice (optional)

450 g (1 lb) haddock or firm white fish, skinned and cut into 2.5-cm (1-in) chunks

125 g (4½ oz) cooked prawns (shrimp), defrosted if frozen

2 Tbsp chopped fresh dill or parsley

Salt and freshly ground black pepper

For the topping

450 g (1 lb) potatoes, peeled and cut into large chunks

225 g (8 oz) sweet potatoes, peeled and cut into large chunks

1 medium courgette (zucchini), trimmed

25 g (2 Tbsp) butter or polyunsaturated margarine

Salt and freshly ground black pepper

Tip: *If you prefer a simple creamed potato topping, cook 675 g (1 lb 8 oz) peeled potatoes, cut into large chunks, in boiling salted water for 15–20 minutes, until tender. Drain thoroughly and mash with 25 g (2 Tbsp) butter or polyunsaturated margarine and 5 tablespoons of semi-skimmed milk. Season with salt and pepper and beat with a wooden spoon for about 1 minute until smooth. Spoon on top of the fish filling and bake for about 20 minutes.*
Nutritional note: *Haddock is a useful source of vitamin B6, a vitamin which helps the body to utilise protein and contributes to the formation of haemoglobin, the pigment in red blood cells.*

❋ Start by making the fish mixture. Put the margarine, flour, stock, milk and lemon juice, if using, in a large saucepan. Slowly bring to the boil, stirring frequently, until the sauce boils and thickens. Simmer for 1 minute, then remove from the heat and stir in the fish, prawns, dill or parsley and seasoning. Spoon the mixture into an ovenproof dish.

❋ To make the topping, put the potatoes and sweet potatoes in a saucepan and pour over just enough boiling water to cover them. Bring back to the boil, then reduce the heat, cover and simmer for 6 minutes. Drain thoroughly and leave to cool for 5 minutes.

❋ Preheat the oven to 180 °C/350 °F/ gas 4. Coarsely grate the potatoes, sweet potato and courgette. Melt the butter or margarine and drizzle over, then season with salt and pepper, and mix together with a fork. Spoon on top of the fish mixture in an even layer. Bake in the oven for about 25 minutes, or until the topping is brown and cooked through.

veg &
pasta

Here, eggs are whisked with a little crème fraîche and thickened into a creamy sauce by the heat of the cooked pasta. Let your child select the pasta at the supermarket; there are plenty of fun shapes to choose from.

Pasta carbonara

SERVES 4

300 g (10½ oz) dried white or wholemeal pasta shapes, e.g. wheels or bows

3 eggs

3 Tbsp crème fraîche or single (light) cream

50 g (2 oz) Parmesan or Cheddar cheese, finely grated

1 Tbsp chopped fresh parsley

Salt and freshly ground black pepper

50 g (2 oz) cooked sliced ham, cut into thin strips

❋ Cook the pasta in a large pan of lightly salted boiling water for 10 minutes, or according to packet instructions, until 'al dente'.

❋ Meanwhile, lightly whisk the eggs together with a fork. Add the crème fraîche or single cream, half the cheese, parsley and a little pepper, if liked. Whisk again.

❋ As soon as the pasta is cooked, turn off the heat, drain the pasta thoroughly and return to the hot pan. Immediately add the egg mixture with the strips of ham. Toss the mixture together well; the eggs will cook in the residual heat to make a sauce. Serve straight away, sprinkled with the remaining cheese.

Tip: 'Al dente' means 'firm to the bite' – pasta should not be soft, but neither should it have a hard, uncooked centre, so test it about a minute before the end of the recommended cooking time.

Variation: Instead of ham, use cooked chicken or turkey cut into bite-size pieces. Left-over or freshly cooked vegetables such as carrot, broccoli or peas, also make a great addition to this dish.

Nutritional note: Pasta is a starchy carbohydrate food, which requires time to be broken down and absorbed by the body, thus raising blood sugar more slowly and less sharply. Pasta provides protein and fibre, especially if using wholemeal varieties.

Brightly coloured crunchy vegetables layered with bread triangles and baked in a savoury cheese custard make this simple supper dish look as good as it tastes.

Cheese and vegetable bake

SERVES 4

1 Tbsp sunflower oil

1 small red onion, peeled and finely chopped

1 stick celery, finely chopped

½ small red or yellow (bell) pepper, de-seeded and finely chopped

75 g (½ cup) frozen peas, defrosted

15 g (1 Tbsp) polyunsaturated margarine

8 slices of thin- or medium-cut white or wholemeal bread

2 eggs

300 ml (1¼ cups) semi-skimmed milk

Salt and freshly ground black pepper

50 g (2 oz) Gruyère or Cheddar cheese, grated

✱ Heat the oil in a large frying pan and gently cook the onion for 5 minutes, until beginning to soften. Add the celery and red or yellow pepper, and cook for a further 5 minutes until almost tender. Remove from the heat and stir in the peas.

✱ Preheat the oven to 160 °C/325 °F/gas 3. Lightly grease a shallow ovenproof dish with the margarine. Trim the crusts from the bread and cut each slice into quarters diagonally. Arrange the bread in overlapping layers in the dish. Spoon the vegetable mixture over the bread. In a bowl, whisk the eggs together with the milk and season with a little salt and pepper. Slowly pour this mixture over the dish, then sprinkle with the cheese. Leave to stand for 5 minutes to soak the bread, then bake for 35–40 minutes, or until the top is golden brown and the savoury custard lightly set.

Tip: *If your children enjoy slightly spicier foods, whisk in a pinch of dry mustard powder or paprika with the egg and milk mixture.*
Nutritional note: *While wholemeal bread is higher in B vitamins and fibre and is great for adults, contrary to popular belief, white bread is good for children and is usually fortified with calcium, so don't worry if they refuse wholemeal bread.*

Here instant polenta is made with vegetable stock for flavour, and milk for extra protein and calcium. When cool, it is cut into slices and topped with grated cheese and grilled.

Polenta with cheese topping

SERVES 4

300 ml (1¼ cups) well-flavoured vegetable stock

450 ml (1¾ cups) semi-skimmed milk

175 g (1 cup) instant polenta (cornmeal)

2 Tbsp chopped fresh parsley

Salt and freshly ground black pepper

125 g (4½ oz) mild or medium Cheddar cheese, grated

1 Tbsp light olive oil

Freshly cooked vegetables, coleslaw or salad, to serve

❉ Grease a 20-cm (8-in) shallow square tin and line the base with baking parchment. Pour the stock and milk into a heavy-based saucepan and bring to the boil. Add the polenta in a steady steam, stirring all the time. Gently cook for 4–5 minutes, or according to the packet instructions, until the mixture is very thick. Stir in the parsley and season to taste. Spoon into the prepared tin and spread out evenly. Leave in a cool place to set for about an hour.

❉ Turn out the set polenta on to a board and remove the lining paper. Cut into 12 rectangles and place on a grill pan. Brush the top with a little of the oil, then cook under a preheated moderately hot grill for 6–7 minutes, until lightly browned. Turn over and brush the tops with the remaining oil. Grill for about 2 minutes, then sprinkle the tops with the cheese and grill for a further 3–4 minutes, or until the cheese has melted and lightly browned. Leave to cool for 2–3 minutes (bubbling cheese can be very hot) before serving with some freshly cooked vegetables, such as peas or broccoli, coleslaw or salad.

Tip: *This polenta (cornmeal) mixture is also delicious made into croutons to serve with soups and casseroles. Stir 50 g (½ cup) grated Cheddar into the mixture, then spread out on a greased baking sheet. When cool, cut into 1-cm (½-in) cubes and grill, turning several times, until lightly browned.*
Nutritional note: *Polenta (cornmeal) is made from ground corn and is the only grain that contains vitamin A, good for healthy eyes and skin and for supporting the immune system.*

This tasty pasta dish is made with an all-in-one sauce. It has a crunchy cheese and crumb topping, but for speed and simplicity, this can be left out.

Easy pasta and cheese sauce

SERVES 4

300 g (10½ oz) dried pasta, such as macaroni

600 ml (2½ cups) semi-skimmed milk

25 g (¼ cup) plain (all-purpose) flour

40 g (3 Tbsp) butter

100 g (3½ oz) medium Cheddar cheese, grated

Salt and freshly ground black pepper

2 tomatoes, thinly sliced

50 g (1 cup) wholemeal breadcrumbs

✱ Cook the pasta in a large pan of lightly salted boiling water for 10 minutes, or according to packet instructions, until 'al dente'.

✱ Meanwhile, pour the milk into a heavy-based saucepan. Add the flour and butter and whisk over a medium heat until the sauce is thick and smooth. Simmer for a further minute. Stir in about two-thirds of the cheese and season to taste with salt and pepper.

✱ Thoroughly drain the pasta and add to the sauce. Mix together well, then transfer to an oven proof dish. Arrange the sliced tomatoes on top, then sprinkle with the breadcrumbs and remaining cheese. Place under a pre-heated moderately hot grill until golden-brown and bubbling. Allow to cool for a minute or two before serving.

Tip: *You may prefer to skin the tomatoes first; put them in a heatproof bowl and pour over enough boiling water to cover. Remove after 45–60 seconds and briefly rinse under cold water; the skins will peel away easily.*

Nutritional note: *Calcium is vital for strong bones and teeth. More than two-thirds of the recommended intake of calcium for 7–10 year olds is supplied by the milk and cheese in this dish.*

Make ahead: *This dish can be made a few hours in advance (don't grill the top), then reheated in an oven preheated to 200 °C/400 °F/gas 6 for about 20 minutes.*

Mixed with rice and vegetables, a small amount of chicken will go a long way. Peperami adds flavour but is quite high in fat, so here it is gently cooked first and the juices from it used to cook the vegetables without the addition of extra oil.

Chicken and pepperoni jambalaya

SERVES 4

50 g (2 oz) Peperami (pepperoni) salami stick, thinly sliced or cut into small cubes

2 chicken breasts, cut into 2cm (¾-in) chunks

1 onion, peeled and chopped

1 celery stick, finely sliced

1 small red (bell) pepper, de-seeded and diced

1–2 garlic cloves, peeled and crushed

½ tsp mild chilli powder

350 g (1¾ cups) long-grain white rice, rinsed

400g (14oz) tin chopped tomatoes, puréed until smooth, if preferred

900 ml (3¾ cups) boiling vegetable stock

Salt and freshly ground black pepper

2 Tbsp chopped fresh parsley

Tip: If preferred, use brown rice instead of white. You will need about 150 ml (⅔ cup) more stock. After adding the tomatoes, stock and seasoning, simmer the mixture for 20 minutes instead of 10.
Nutritional note: Garlic contains a phytochemical known as allicin, which has both anti-fungal and antibiotic properties. It is thought to be beneficial for both prevention and for faster recovery of colds and chest infections.

❊ Heat a large non-stick saucepan over a moderately high heat for a minute, add the Peperami and cook, turning frequently for 3–4 minutes until the fat runs out. Remove the Peperami with a slotted spoon and set aside. Add the chicken to the pan and cook for 2–3 minutes until lightly coloured. Remove and add to the Peperami, leaving any fat and juices behind. If the pan is now dry, add just a little sunflower or olive oil.

❊ Turn down the heat a little and cook the onion for 3–4 minutes, stirring occasionally. Stir in the celery, red pepper, garlic and chilli powder, cook for a minute, then stir in the rice, followed by the tomatoes and stock. Season with a little salt and pepper. Bring to the boil, then reduce the heat so that the mixture is simmering gently. Cover the pan with a tight-fitting lid and cook for 10 minutes.

❊ Stir in the chicken, Peperami and parsley. Re-cover and cook for a further 7–8 minutes, or until the chicken is cooked and the rice is tender and has absorbed most of the stock. Leave to stand for a few minutes before serving.

Colourful and fresh-tasting, stir-fries are quick and healthy. This is a simplified version of chow mein, made with juicy prawns and topped with wafer-thin strands of omelette.

Simple prawn stir-fry

SERVES 4

300 g (10½ oz) egg thread noodles or rice noodles

2 Tbsp groundnut or sunflower oil

2 eggs, lightly beaten

Salt and freshly ground black pepper

1 garlic clove, peeled and crushed

200 g (3 cups) bean sprouts

125 g (4½ oz) Chinese leaf (cabbagge), shredded

225 g (8 oz) cooked prawns (shrimp), defrosted if frozen

3 Tbsp soy sauce

1 Tbsp tomato paste

Pinch caster (superfine) sugar

✳ Cook the noodles in a large saucepan with plenty of boiling water and 1 teaspoon of the oil, according to packet instructions. Drain and set aside.

✳ Meanwhile, heat 2 teaspoons of the oil in a large non-stick frying pan. In a bowl, lightly beat the eggs and season with a little salt and pepper, pour into the pan and swirl to coat the base thinly. Cook for 1 minute, or until very lightly browned, then flip over and cook for a further 30 seconds. Turn out onto a board and roll up the omelette tightly.

✳ Heat the remaining 1 tablespoon of oil in the pan. Add the garlic, bean sprouts and Chinese leaf and cook over a high heat for 3 minutes, stirring all the time. Stir in the prawns and cooked noodles. In a bowl, stir the soy sauce, tomato paste and sugar together with 2 tablespoons of cold water. Add to the pan, toss together well and cook for a further 2 minutes until heated through. Turn off the heat and cover with a lid. Finely slice the rolled up omelette, then spoon the stir-fry onto warmed plates and scatter with the fine strips of omelette. Serve straight away.

Variation: *For a vegetarian version, use a 250-g (9-oz) packet of plain or smoked tofu, cut into 2-cm (¾-in) cubes, instead of the prawns (shrimp).*
Nutritional note: *Prawns (shrimp) are rich in zinc and selenium, both of which are essential for a strong immune system and speed up healing.*

Here, a tasty vegetable mixture in a creamy sauce is given a fluffly cheese soufflé topping. Children love individual servings and these are sure to please.

Vegetable surprise

SERVES 4

- 25 g (2 Tbsp) polyunsaturated margarine
- 1 garlic clove, peeled and crushed
- 6 spring onions (scallions), thinly sliced
- 1 tsp plain (all-purpose) flour
- 200 ml (¾ cup) semi-skimmed milk
- 100 g (1 cup) frozen mixed vegetables, defrosted
- Salt and freshly ground black pepper
- 100 g (3½ oz) Cheddar cheese, finely grated
- 50 g (1 cup) wholemeal breadcrumbs
- 2 eggs, separated

✻ Preheat the oven to 200 °C/400 °F/gas 6. Use about one third of the margarine to lightly grease four 150-ml (⅔-cup) ramekin dishes and put them on a baking tray. Melt the remaining margarine in a small heavy-based saucepan. Add the garlic and spring onions and cook gently for 3–4 minutes until soft. Sprinkle over the flour, cook for a few seconds, then turn off the heat. Gradually stir in half the milk, then return to the heat and bring to the boil. Stir in the vegetables and season with salt and pepper. Divide the mixture between the prepared ramekins.

✻ Mix together the rest of the milk, cheese, breadcrumbs and egg yolks. Whisk the egg whites until stiff and fold into the mixture, half at a time. Spoon the cheese mixture on top of the vegetables. Bake for 15 minutes, until well-risen and golden brown. Serve at once.

Tip: *If you can't serve straight away, leave the ramekins in the oven with the door slightly ajar; they'll stay puffy for a few minutes.*
Nutritional note: *Many frozen vegetables have higher levels of nutrients than 'fresh' vegetables. This is because they are usually processed and frozen very quickly after being picked.*

It can be difficult to persuade children to eat a variety of vegetables, so here a potato pastry tart is filled with roasted vegetables, which have been puréed until smooth.

Mediterranean vegetable tart

SERVES 4

For the potato pastry

300 g (10½ oz) potatoes, peeled and cut into chunks

1½ Tbsp semi-skimmed milk

½ tsp dried mixed herbs

125 g (1 cup) plain (all-purpose) flour

Pinch of salt

50 g (¼ cup) diced chilled butter or polyunsaturated margarine

For the vegetable topping

350 g (12½ oz) butternut squash, peeled, de-seeded and cubed

1 red onion, peeled and quartered

2 cloves of garlic, unpeeled

1 red (bell) pepper, quartered and de-seeded

2 Tbsp olive oil

50 g (2 oz) Cheddar cheese, grated

✽ Start by preparing the pastry. Cook the potatoes in lightly salted boiling water for 15 minutes, or until tender. Drain thoroughly, then return to the pan and mash with the milk and herbs. Leave to cool.

✽ Preheat the oven to 200 °C/400 °F/gas 6. To make the topping, put the butternut squash cubes, onion, garlic and pepper on a baking tray and drizzle with the oil. Toss to coat. Bake on the middle shelf of the oven for 15 minutes.

✽ Meanwhile, place the potato pastry on a non-stick baking sheet and roll out to a 25-cm (10-in) round. Fold over about 1 cm (½ in) of the edges, then crimp or mark a pattern with a fork. Turn the vegetables over and place the potato flan case on the top shelf of the oven. Bake both for 20 minutes, then remove both from the oven.

✽ Allow the roasted vegetable to cool for a few minutes. Place in a food processor (remove the garlic skins first) and blend until smooth. Spoon the vegetable purée over the flan case, sprinkle with the cheese and bake for 15 minutes. Cut into wedges to serve.

Tip: *Check the vegetables towards the end of cooking time and turn more frequently if the edges are starting to char.*
Nutritional note: *Pastry alternatives like this potato pastry add variety and nutrients to your child's diet and are also lower in fat.*

Children will love these moist turkey meatballs. Simmered in a smooth tomato sauce with rice, the only accompaniment needed for this all-in-one dish is a few steamed green beans, peas or sweetcorn.

Turkey meatballs and rice

SERVES 4

25 g (1 oz) white or wholemeal bread, crusts removed

2 Tbsp milk

225 g (8 oz) minced turkey

1 small carrot, about 50 g (2 oz), peeled and finely grated

1 garlic clove, peeled and crushed

Salt and freshly ground black pepper, to taste

400-g (14-oz) tin plum tomatoes

2 tsp sun-dried tomato paste

350 ml (1½ cups) chicken or vegetable stock

1 bay leaf

100 g (½ cup) easy-cook white rice, rinsed

1 Tbsp fresh or frozen chopped parsley

✷ Cut the bread into small cubes and put in a mixing bowl. Sprinkle over the milk and leave to soak for 5 minutes. Add the turkey, carrot and garlic, then season with salt and pepper if liked. Shape the mixture into 20 small balls and set aside.

✷ Tip the plum tomatoes into a blender or food processor. Add the tomato paste and purée until smooth. Pour into a large, heavy-based saucepan. Add the stock and bay leaf and bring to the boil. Stir in the rice and cook briskly for 5 minutes, then reduce the heat to a gentle simmer. Carefully drop in the meatballs, cover the pan and simmer for a further 8–10 minutes, or until both the meatballs and rice are cooked.

✷ Remove the bay leaf, stir in the parsley, taste and adjust the seasoning if necessary. Spoon onto warmed plates and serve straight away with freshly cooked vegetables and slices of Italian-style bread such as focaccia or ciabatta for larger appetites.

Tip: *The meatballs may be made up to 24 hours before cooking. Shape and place on baking parchment (or they will stick) on a plate, then cover and keep refrigerated. You could also make double quantity and freeze half. Open-freeze the raw meatballs on a non-stick baking tray, then transfer to a freezer container. Separate and defrost overnight in the refrigerator or for 2 hours at room temperature.*

This colourful dish is simple to make and ideal for a nutritious mid-week meal. It can be made with either freshly-cooked or leftover rice.

Special fried rice

MAKES 20

2 Tbsp groundnut or sunflower oil

3 eggs, lightly beaten

Salt and pepper

125 g (4½ oz) lean pork, e.g. fillet, cut into small dice

4 spring onions (scallions), finely sliced

1 Tbsp soy sauce

450 g (3½ cups) cooked white or brown rice

75 g (2½ oz) cooked prawns (shrimp), defrosted if frozen

125 g (1 cup) frozen peas, defrosted

2 Tbsp vegetable stock or water

✲ Heat 1 tablespoon of the oil in a large frying pan or wok, preferably non-stick, over a moderate heat. In a bowl, season the eggs with a little salt and pepper (don't over-season as the soy sauce is salty), add to the pan and cook for about half a minute, stirring constantly until lightly scrambled. Remove from the pan and set aside. If necessary, wipe the pan clean with kitchen paper.

✲ Pour the remaining oil into the pan and turn up the heat to moderately hot. Add the pork and onions and cook over a high heat for a minute, or until the meat is lightly browned and the onion soft. Sprinkle over the soy sauce, then stir in the cooked rice, prawns, peas and stock or water. Lower the heat a little and cook, stirring frequently for 3–4 minutes. Add the scrambled egg and cook for a few more seconds to warm through, then serve straight away.

Tip: *The weight of rice increases about two and a half times during cooking, so if using uncooked rice for this dish you'll need a little more than 175 g (¾ cup).*
Nutritional note: *Rapid growth coupled with poor dietary choices can result in iron-deficiency, which in turn can cause fatigue and affect academic performance. Peas are one of a few vegetables that are a good source of iron and are just as nutritious frozen as fresh. They also contain vitamin C, which helps the body absorb this vital mineral.*

In most dishes, a sauce and pasta are cooked separately and then combined. In this all-in-one dish, the pasta is cooked in a well-flavoured stock with cream cheese and chopped vegetables, creating a delicious sauce.

Saucy salmon and pasta

SERVES 4

15 g (1 Tbsp) butter or polyunsaturated margarine

50 g (2 oz) button mushrooms, quartered

125 g (½ cup) cream cheese

600 ml (2½ cups) well-flavoured vegetable stock

300 g (10½ oz) dried pasta shapes

75 g (2½ oz) fine green beans, trimmed and cut into 2.5-cm (1-in) lengths

200-g (7-oz) tin pink salmon, drained and flaked

Salt and freshly ground black pepper, to taste

❋ Melt the butter or margarine in a large saucepan. Add the mushrooms and cook over a medium heat for 3–4 minutes, or until just beginning to brown. Add the cream cheese and stir until melted, then gradually add the stock. Bring to the boil.

❋ Add the pasta to the stock and bring back to the boil. Reduce the stock to a gentle boil, half-cover the pan with a lid and cook for 6 minutes. Add the beans and cook for a further 4 minutes, or until the pasta and beans are just cooked. Turn off the heat, then gently stir in the salmon and season with salt and pepper, if liked. Cover and allow to stand for a minute before serving.

Tip: *When cooking the pasta, make sure that it is gently boiling; the liquid should bubble up just above the pasta, but take care not to let it boil over.*
Variation: *Instead of salmon, use tinned tuna, or cooked chicken or ham, cut into strips. Left-over cooked or defrosted frozen peas or sweetcorn may be used instead of green beans; add them a minute or two before the end of cooking.*
Nutritional note: *Salmon, including the tinned variety, is a great source of essential fats that support the immune system and brain function. Try to encourage your child (and the rest of the family) to enjoy oily fish at least once a week.*

Most children love sausages. Instead of serving them with fries or mash, add them to this colourful rice and vegetable dish for a change.

Mini sausage pilaf

SERVES 4

20 pork cocktail sausages

1 tsp olive oil

15 g (1 Tbsp) butter, preferably unsalted

1 small onion, peeled and finely chopped

2 rashers streaky bacon, rind removed, chopped

1 garlic clove, peeled and crushed

175 g (¾ cup) easy-cook basmati rice, rinsed

600 ml (2½ cups) vegetable stock

4 ripe tomatoes, skinned, seeded and chopped

125 g (1 cup) frozen peas, defrosted

200g (7oz) tin red kidney beans, drained

2 Tbsp chopped parsley

Salt and freshly ground black pepper, to taste

✽ Grill the sausages under a medium-hot grill for 7–8 minutes, turning frequently until they are lightly browned all over. Place them on a plate lined with absorbent kitchen paper and blot them to remove the excess fat.

✽ Heat the oil and butter in a large saucepan, preferably non-stick, until sizzling. Add the onion and bacon and gently sauté for 4–5 minutes, then add the garlic and cook for a further minute, stirring all the time. Add the rice and stir to coat in the juices, then pour in the stock. Cover the pan with a lid and simmer for 10 minutes.

✽ Stir the sausages, tomatoes, peas, kidney beans and parsley into the mixture. Season with salt and pepper and simmer, uncovered, for a further 6–7 minutes, or until the rice is tender and most of the liquid has been absorbed. Turn off the heat and cover the pan with the lid. Leave to stand for 2–3 minutes before serving.

Tip: *Skin the tomatoes by placing in a heat-proof bowl and covering with boiling water. Leave to stand for 45 seconds. Drain and rinse briefly under cold water to cool. The skins should be easy to peel off.*
Nutritional note: *Choose good-quality, high-meat-content sausages for this dish. Pork is an extremely good source of nutrients and contains large amounts of B vitamins, particularly niacin and B12. Vitamin B12 is vital for the production of red blood cells and normal growth.*

Crumbles don't have to be sweet as this tasty savoury dish shows. Ideal as a vegetable main course, you could also halve the quantities and serve it as an accompaniment to grilled meat such as chicken breasts or sausages.

Creamy vegetable crumble

SERVES 4

For the topping

100 g (1 cup) wholemeal flour

50 g (¼ cup) butter or polyunsaturated margarine, cubed

75 g (2½ oz) Cheddar or red Leicester cheese, grated

50 g (⅓ cup) almonds or cashew nuts, coarsely chopped

1 Tbsp sunflower seeds

For the filling

25 g (2 Tbsp) butter or polyunsaturated margarine

2 medium leeks, sliced

1 carrot, peeled and sliced

1 stick celery, sliced

125 g (4½ oz) baby button mushrooms

350 g (12½ oz) sweet potatoes, peeled and cut into 2-cm (¾-in) cubes

1 Tbsp plain (all-purpose) flour

150 ml (⅔ cup) vegetable stock

Salt and freshly ground black pepper

75 g (⅓ cup) mascarpone or cream cheese

✳ Preheat the oven to 180 °C/350 °F/gas 4. Start by making the topping. Put the flour and butter or margarine in a bowl and rub together until the mixture resembles fine breadcrumbs. Stir in the cheese, nuts and seeds, and set aside.

✳ To make the filling, melt the butter or margarine in a heavy-based saucepan. Add the leeks, stir to coat, then cover and cook for 3 minutes. Remove the lid and stir in the remaining vegetables. Cook for a further 5 minutes, stirring frequently. Sprinkle the flour over the vegetables and stir to blend into the juices, then gradually stir in the stock and season with salt and pepper. Bring to the boil and simmer for a minute until thickened, then add the mascarpone or cream cheese and stir until melted. Tip the mixture into a shallow oven-proof dish, then sprinkle over the crumble topping. Bake for 35–40 minutes, or until the vegetables are tender and the topping is golden-brown. Allow to cool for a few minutes before serving.

Tips: *Vary the vegetables if you like, but try to keep the quantity about the same. Try different root vegetables such as potatoes, baby turnips or swede (rutabaga).*
❄ *If you are using polyunsaturated margarine chill it first in the freezer for about 10 minutes before rubbing into the flour.*

Nutritional note: *The combination of cheese, nuts and seeds adds plenty of protein to this dish for vegetarians. Seeds are packed full of concentrated nutrients for the benefit of the potential plants; as well as containing an assortment of vitamins and minerals, they are a rich source of essential fats.*

This is a child-friendly version of 'salade niçoise' but without the anchovies and olives. Serve with crusty French bread for those with larger appetites.

Summer salad

SERVES 4

For the salad

225 g (8 oz) even-sized, waxy new potatoes, scrubbed

175 g (6 oz) thin green beans, halved

3 eggs, at room temperature

1 Little Gem lettuce, torn into tiny pieces, or finely shredded

¼ cucumber, peeled and thinly sliced

125g (4½ oz) baby plum tomatoes, halved

185g (6½ oz) tin tuna in oil, drained and flaked

For the dressing

2 Tbsp light olive or sunflower oil

2 tsp red or white wine vinegar

¼ tsp Dijon mustard (optional)

Pinch of caster (superfine) sugar

Salt and freshly ground black pepper

✤ Cook the potatoes in salted boiling water for 12–15 minutes, or until tender, adding the beans for the last 5 minutes of cooking time. Remove from the pan with a slotted spoon and transfer to a bowl. Add the eggs to the hot water, bring back to the boil and simmer for 7–8 minutes. Cool in cold water, remove the shells and cut each into quarters, lengthways.

✤ While the eggs are cooking, make the dressing by whisking all the ingredients in a small bowl or by shaking together in a screw-topped jar. Cut the warm potatoes in half or quarters if large. Pour the dressing over the potatoes and beans and toss to coat. Leave to cool completely.

✤ Add the lettuce, cucumber, tomatoes and tuna to the potatoes and bean mixture and gently toss together, taking care not to break up the tuna too much. Divide between four serving plates, then arrange the hard-boiled egg quarters on top. Serve straight away with French bread.

Nutritional note: *Tinned tuna retains most of the vitamins, minerals and omega 3 fatty acids that are in fresh tuna. Omega 3 helps keep the heart healthy and is believed to improve concentration levels in some children.*

Tinned tuna makes an inexpensive meal and – apart from fish fingers – is one fish that most children like. Here it is combined with a tomato sauce and used as a filling for cannelloni.

Tuna cannelloni

SERVES 4

1 Tbsp light olive oil

1 onion, peeled and finely chopped

1 garlic clove, peeled and crushed

400 g (14 oz) tin chopped tomatoes

185-g (6½-oz) tin tuna, drained and flaked

½ tsp dried mixed herbs

Salt and freshly ground black pepper

12 cannelloni tubes

15 g (1 Tbsp) butter or polyunsaturated margarine

15 g (2 Tbsp) plain (all-purpose) flour

450 ml (1¾ cups) semi-skimmed milk

Pinch of freshly grated nutmeg (optional)

75 g (2½ oz) medium Cheddar cheese, grated

✶ Heat the oil in a heavy-based saucepan, add the onion and gently cook for 7–8 minutes, until almost soft. Stir in the garlic and cook for a few seconds, then add the chopped tomatoes (purée them first if your child doesn't like lumps of tomatoes). Bring to the boil and simmer for 15 minutes, or until the sauce has reduced slightly and is thick. Remove from the heat and allow to cool for about 5 minutes, then stir in the tuna and herbs. Season to taste with salt and pepper. Spoon the filling into the cannelloni tubes and arrange in a single layer in a lightly greased ovenproof dish.

✶ Preheat the oven to 190 °C/375 °F/gas 5. To make the cheese sauce, put the margarine, flour and milk into a saucepan and bring to the boil, whisking all the time until smooth and thickened. Season with salt and pepper and nutmeg if liked, then stir in half the cheese. Pour the sauce over the cannelloni, sprinkle the top with the remaining cheese and bake for 35 minutes, or until golden and bubbling. Cool for a few minutes before serving with a salad or some steamed green vegetables.

Tip: *Look out for tinned tomatoes with additions like herbs and onions. They add flavour and make food preparation faster while costing only a little more.*
Nutritional note: *Although this recipe is made with only one tin of tuna, there's plenty of additional protein provided by the milk and cheese.*

Here, mini meatballs are cooked in a bolognaise sauce with some tiny diced vegetables. Most children love spaghetti but it can be messy to eat, so for young ones, break it into manageable lengths before cooking.

Spaghetti with meatballs

SERVES 4

450 g (1 lb) extra lean minced beef

1 garlic clove, peeled and crushed

1 tsp dried mixed herbs

Salt and freshly ground black pepper, to taste

2 Tbsp olive oil

1 onion, peeled and finely chopped

1 carrot, peeled and finely diced

1 medium courgette (zucchini), trimmed and finely diced

400 g (14 oz) tin chopped tomatoes

1 Tbsp tomato paste

300 ml (1¼ cups) beef stock

350 g (12½ oz) dried spaghetti

Finely grated cheese, to serve

✳ Put the minced beef, garlic and herbs in a large bowl with salt and pepper to taste and mix thoroughly until combined. Using slightly wet hands roll the mixture into 24 small meatballs. Heat 1 tablespoon of the oil in a large frying pan and fry half the meatballs over a medium-high heat for 5–6 minutes, until browned all over. Remove with a slotted spoon, leaving the oil and juices behind, and transfer to a plate lined with absorbent kitchen paper. Cook the remaining meatballs in the same way. Set aside.

✳ Add the remaining oil to the pan and gently cook the onion for 5 minutes, until soft. Add the carrot, courgette, chopped tomatoes, paste and stock. Season to taste. Bring to the boil, cover and simmer for 15 minutes. Add the meatballs and simmer for a further 10 minutes, or until the meatballs are tender and the sauce reduced.

✳ Meanwhile, add the spaghetti to a large saucepan of boiling salted water and cook according to packet instructions. Drain the spaghetti and divide among individual plates. Spoon the meatballs and sauce onto the pasta and serve sprinkled with some grated cheese.

Nutritional note: *Beef is a good source of iron, needed for both physical and mental development. To improve its absorption, follow the meal with some vitamin C-rich fruit or serve with a glass of orange or cranberry juice.*

Tip: *If you have time, make a 'face' on the top of the salad with a couple of large grapes for eyes, a triangle of the cheese for a nose and a slice of apple for a smiley mouth. Arrange the croutons on the top of the salad as hair.*

Nutritional note: *Both apples and grapes contain fructose, a simple sugar that is released slowly to supply the body with energy and help balance blood sugar levels. They are also great for healthy skin.*

Children will often eat salad if the ingredients are finely chopped and attractively presented. This combination of fruit, vegetables, cheese and croutons makes a well-balanced meal all on its own.

Cheese salad with croutons

SERVES 2

For the salad

¼ iceberg lettuce, 1 lettuce heart or a handful of salad leaves, finely shredded or torn into small pieces

1 celery stick, thinly sliced

75 g (½ cup) seedless black grapes, halved if large

75 g (2½ oz) Edam, Gouda or mild Cheddar cheese, cut into 1-cm (½in) cubes

1 red eating (dessert) apple

1 Tbsp orange juice

2 slices white or wholemeal bread

15 g (1 Tbsp) polyunsaturated margarine

For the yoghurt and honey dressing

1 Tbsp orange juice

1 Tbsp walnut or sunflower oil

2 tsp clear honey

5 Tbsp plain bio yoghurt

Salt and freshly ground black pepper

✳ Put the lettuce, celery, grapes and cheese in a large bowl. Quarter, core and chop the apple into bite-sized pieces, then toss in the orange juice to prevent them from browning. Add to the bowl, then gently toss everything together.

✳ Thinly spread both sides of the bread with the margarine. Trim the crusts, then cut into 1-cm (½-in) cubes. Heat a large heavy-based non-stick frying pan over a moderate heat, then add the bread cubes and cook, turning frequently, for 5–6 minutes, or until golden and crisp. Remove from the pan and set aside.

✳ For the dressing, whisk together the orange juice, oil and honey in a small bowl or jug with a fork, then whisk in the yoghurt, a little at a time. Season with salt and pepper. Drizzle half over the salad and toss well. Divide between two plates, then drizzle with the remaining dressing and scatter with the croutons. Serve straight away.

desserts

Although there's no cream in this recipe, it has a lovely flavour and the combination of egg yolks and skimmed milk powder give it an amazingly creamy texture.

Vanilla ice cream

**MAKES 1 LITRE
(4 CUPS)**

300 ml (1¼ cups) whole milk

25 g (¼ cup) skimmed milk powder

75 g (⅓ cup) caster (superfine) sugar, preferably unrefined

3 egg yolks

1 tsp cornflour (cornstarch)

1 tsp vanilla extract

✽ Warm the milk, milk powder and 1 tablespoon of the sugar to boiling point, stirring occasionally. Meanwhile, using an electric whisk, beat the egg yolks, remaining sugar, cornflour and vanilla in a heatproof bowl, until thick and pale. Gradually whisk in the boiling milk. Pour the mixture back into the pan and bring back to boiling point, stirring, until thickened. Tip back into the bowl, cover the surface directly with damp greaseproof paper and leave to cool.

✽ Churn the mixture in an ice cream maker, according to the manufacturer's instructions, until frozen. Transfer to a freezer container, cover the surface directly with greaseproof paper and store in the freezer for up to one month.

Tip: *See the method on page 142 for making ice cream without an ice cream maker.*
Variations: *For strawberry ice cream, blend 225 g (1½ cups) strawberries, rinsed and hulled, to a purée. Pass the purée through a fine sieve to remove the seeds, if preferred. Stir the purée into the vanilla custard before churning.*
✽ *To make chocolate ice cream, add 2 tablespoons of sifted unsweetened cocoa powder to the egg yolk, sugar and cornflour (cornstarch) mixture.*
✽ *For ice cream sundaes, make a fresh fruit sauce by blending 225 g (8 oz) prepared fresh fruit, such as raspberries or kiwi fruit, in a food processor. Add 1 teaspoon of lemon juice and blend to a purée, then press through a fine sieve placed over a bowl. Discard the seeds. Stir in 1–2 tablespoons of sifted icing (confectioners') sugar. Chill until needed (the sauce will keep for 2–3 days in the refrigerator). Place 2 or 3 small scoops of different flavoured ice creams into a sundae glass, layering with fresh or canned fruit if you like, then drizzle with fresh fruit sauce. Serve immediately.*

With a moist texture and rich chocolate flavour, these are ideal for vegans and those with a food intolerance or an allergy to dairy produce or eggs. Few will be able to detect any difference between these and 'regular' chocolate muffins.

Double chocolate muffins

MAKES 9

50 g (2 oz) creamed coconut

300 ml (1¼ cups) boiling water

5 Tbsp sunflower oil

225 g (2 cups) self-raising flour

25 g (¼ cup) unsweetened cocoa powder

1 tsp baking powder

100 g (½ cup) light brown sugar

75 g (2½ oz) dairy-free chocolate or carob chips

❉ Preheat the oven to 200 °C/400 °F/gas 6. Grease a 9-hole muffin tray or line with paper muffin cases. Roughly chop the creamed coconut. Add to the boiling water in a jug and stir until dissolved. Add the oil, then leave the mixture until tepid.

❉ Sift the flour, cocoa and baking powders into a mixing bowl. Stir in the sugar and chocolate or carob chips. Add the coconut mixture and briefly mix until just combined, but still a little lumpy.

❉ Divide the mixture between the prepared muffin tray or cases and place in the oven. Immediately turn down the oven temperature to 180 °C/350 °F/gas 4 and bake for 16–18 minutes, until well-risen and firm. Leave the muffins in the tin for a few minutes, then carefully transfer to a wire rack. Serve warm or cold.

Tips: *Make sure you use hard block creamed coconut for these muffins. Don't use tinned creamed coconut, which is a thick liquid and would be unsuitable for this recipe.*
❉ *Heating the oven to a slightly higher temperature gives the muffins an initial blast of heat to help them rise; don't forget to turn the oven down to the lower setting after adding them.*
Nutritional note: *Sunflower oil is almost tasteless which makes it ideal for baking. Extracted from the seeds of the sunflower, it is very high in polyunsaturated fat and low in saturated fat, unlike butter, which is often used to make muffins.*

In hot weather ice lollies are a real treat for kids, but shop-bought varieties are often low in nutrients. These frozen strawberry treats are made with fresh fruit and taste delicious, too!

Strawberry ice lollies

MAKES 6

225 g (1½ cups) fresh strawberries

125 ml (½ cup) thick natural yoghurt

3 Tbsp clear honey

❊ Set the freezer to rapid freeze. Rinse out 6 ice lolly moulds with cold water. Hull the strawberries, then briefly rinse in cold water and pat dry on absorbent kitchen paper. Roughly chop and put in a blender or food processor with the yoghurt and honey. Blend until smooth. Carefully pour the mixture into the ice lolly moulds (if you've used a food processor rather than a blender, you may find it easier to pour the mixture into a jug first). Push an ice lolly stick or handle top into each, then freeze for at least 4 hours until solid. Eat within a week of making.

Variations: *Lollies can be made with all sorts of fruit purées. Try other berries such as blackberries and raspberries (sieve after blending to remove the pips), or melons or mangoes. Lollies can also be simply made with pure fruit juice such as orange, tropical fruit or apple.*
Tip: *If the strawberries are really sweet and ripe, you can reduce the amount of honey a little.*
Nutritional note: *Strawberries contain a phytochemical called ellagic acid, which helps protect against cancer. Strawberries are also a great source of vitamin C which is vital for the formation of collagen (a protein needed for healthy bones, teeth, gums and all connective tissue).*

V

This mousse is made from just a few simple ingredients: chocolate, orange juice and water. Whisking the melted mixture over chilled water gives it a fluffy texture. Serve in small portions. Keeps for up to two days in the refrigerator.

Chocolate and orange whip

MAKES 20

200 g (7 oz) milk chocolate

Freshly squeezed juice of 2 oranges

❋ Break up the chocolate into small pieces and put it in a heavy-based saucepan. Pour the orange juice into a jug and make up to 175 ml (¾ cup) with water. Add this to the chocolate. Gently heat until the chocolate has completely melted, stirring now and then. Remove from the heat and leave to cool.

❋ Put ice and water into a larger bowl, then place a smaller bowl in it. Pour the melted mixture into the smaller bowl, then whisk with an electric whisk for 5 minutes, until the mousse has the texture of lightly whipped cream (don't over-whip, as the mixture will thicken further and set as it chills). Spoon into individual dishes and chill in the refrigerator until ready to serve.

Tip: *Heat the chocolate and juice very gently, making sure that the mixture doesn't become too hot as vitamin C is destroyed by heat.*
Nutritional note: *While chocolate is high in sugar and fat, it's not all bad news. It also contains immune-boosting antioxidants and iron – the vitamin C in the orange juice will help the body to absorb this.*

This is an incredibly simple dessert, which can be cooked alongside a main course to make the most of your oven. Baking bananas in their skins intensifies their sweetness, so don't be tempted to over-do the chocolate.

Sticky chocolate bananas

SERVES 4

4 medium-sized just ripe bananas, unpeeled

100 g (3½ oz) milk or plain (semisweet) chocolate, roughly chopped

Greek or thick plain yoghurt, to serve

✽ Preheat the oven to 180 °C/350 °F/gas 4. Make a cut along the length of the unpeeled bananas, cutting through the skin, then open up and press the chocolate pieces into the banana flesh.

✽ Wrap each banana in foil, keeping the cut-side uppermost, then place on a baking tray and bake for 12–15 minutes, or until the banana is soft and the chocolate has melted. Leave to cool for 5 minutes before serving with Greek or thick plain yoghurt.

Variation: *For baked pears with white chocolate, cut 2 large ripe pears in half lengthways and scoop out the core using a teaspoon or melon baller. Brush the cut side with orange or lemon juice to prevent it from browning. Mix 50 g (2 oz) finely chopped white chocolate with 1 crushed digestive biscuit (Graham Cracker) and 1 tablespoon of honey, then divide the mixture between the pear halves, spooning it into mounds where the cores have been removed. Loosely wrap each in foil, then bake on a baking tray for 15 minutes until the pears are tender and the filling melted.*
Nutritional note: *Bananas have a high potassium content. This mineral is especially vital for the functioning of nerves and muscles, but is also needed by all cells in the body.*

Raspberries and cream are one of the true delights of summer. Here, creamy bio yoghurt replaces most of the cream to make a lower-fat mousse and just a little whipping cream is folded in to lighten the texture.

Raspberry yoghurt mousse

SERVES 4

1 Tbsp powdered gelatine

3 Tbsp cold water

350 g (2¾ cups) fresh raspberries

1–2 Tbsp caster (superfine) sugar

300 ml (1¼ cups) plain or vanilla low-fat bio yoghurt

100 ml (scant ½ cup) whipping cream, preferably half-fat

✽ Sprinkle the gelatine over the cold water in a small bowl and leave to soak for 5 minutes. Place the bowl over a pan of near-boiling water, leave for 2–3 minutes, then stir until the gelatine has dissolved. Cool for 5 minutes.

✽ Meanwhile, set aside four raspberries for decoration. Put the remaining raspberries in a separate bowl, sprinkle over the sugar and mash with a fork. Stir in the dissolved gelatine, then blend in the yoghurt. In another bowl, whisk the cream until soft peaks form, then gently fold into the yoghurt mixture. Divide between four serving dishes and chill in the refrigerator for at least 2 hours, or until softly set. Decorate the mousse with the reserved fresh raspberries just before serving.

Tip: *Always add gelatine to liquid and not the other way around (otherwise it will stick together in a big lump!). Take care when dissolving not to let the water boil or the gelatine won't set properly. Vegetarian gelatine may be used for this recipe; follow the instructions on the packet carefully.*
Nutritional note: *Bio yoghurts have a mild, creamy taste and contain live bacteria which are beneficial to the digestive system.*

A cross between an ice cream and a sorbet, this frozen dessert has a lovely fruity flavour and a deliciously smooth creamy texture. Make sure you use 'real' apple juice and not a drink made from apple juice concentrate.

Apple and yoghurt sherbet

**MAKES ABOUT
600 ML (2½ CUPS)**

450 ml (1¾ cups)
apple juice

Finely pared strip of
unwaxed lemon rind

100 g (½ cup) caster
(superfine) sugar

200 ml (¾ cup)
Greek yoghurt

❉ Put 150 ml (⅔ cup) of the apple juice, lemon rind and sugar in a saucepan and slowly bring to the boil, stirring occasionally, to dissolve the sugar. Reduce the heat and simmer for 3 minutes. Allow to cool completely, then discard the lemon rind.

❉ Whisk the Greek yoghurt into the cooled syrup, then stir in the remaining apple juice. Pour the mixture into an ice cream maker and churn, according to the manufacturer's instructions, until frozen. Serve immediately or transfer to a freezer container, and freeze for up to two to three weeks.

Tips: *If you don't have an ice cream maker, transfer the mixture to a suitable freezer container, cover and place in the coldest part of your freezer for about 1½ hours, or until the sides and base are just frozen and the middle, slushy. Remove from the freezer and beat using an electric or hand whisk, to break up the large ice crystals. Return to the freezer and repeat this process twice more. Finally, allow the sherbet to freeze for at least 2 hours.*
❉ *Fruity sherbets and sorbets taste wonderful with even more fruit puréed into a sauce. Blend together 225 g (1½ cups) blackberries or raspberries with 2 tablespoons of icing (confectioners') sugar in a food processor until smooth. Sieve to remove the pips and use the sauce within a day of making, or freeze for up to two weeks, then defrost for 2 hours at room temperature or overnight in the refrigerator.*
Variation: *For mango and lime yoghurt sherbet, make the syrup as before using 150 ml (⅔ cup) water and a strip of lime rind instead of lemon. Peel and roughly chop the flesh of 1 ripe mango and purée with the juice of 1 lime. Use this purée instead of apple juice. Freeze for up to 2–3 weeks.*
Nutritional note: *Apple juice contains fructose, a simple sugar that is released slowly to supply the body with energy and help balance blood sugar levels.*

These individual chocolate sponges can be made in single-portion pudding basins or ramekin dishes. Here, they are served with a home-made egg custard, but you can use shop-bought custard or some thick yoghurt if you prefer.

Chocolate castle puddings

MAKES 4

For the sponge

- 40 g (3 Tbsp) golden caster (superfine) sugar
- 40 g (3 Tbsp) polyunsaturated margarine
- 25 g (¼ cup) wholemeal self-raising flour
- 15 g (1 Tbsp) white self-raising flour
- 15 g (2 Tbsp) unsweetened cocoa powder
- 1 egg, lightly beaten
- 25 g (1 oz) plain (semisweet), milk or white chocolate chips

For the custard

- 300 ml (1¼ cups) semi-skimmed milk
- 2 egg yolks
- 1 Tbsp caster (superfine) sugar
- 2 tsp cornflour (cornstarch)
- 1 tsp vanilla extract

❊ Preheat the oven to 180 °C/350 °F/gas 4. Lightly grease four 150-ml (5-fl oz) single-portion pudding basins or ramekins and line the base of each with a small circle of baking parchment. To make the sponge, put the sugar and margarine in a mixing bowl and beat together until blended. Sift over the flours and cocoa powder, adding any bran left in the sieve. Add the egg and beat for a minute until the mixture is light. Beat in the chocolate chips. Divide the mixture between the prepared dishes, place on a baking sheet and bake in the oven for 15 minutes, until well-risen and firm.

❊ Meanwhile, make the custard. Pour the milk into a heavy-based saucepan and heat until just starting to simmer. In a bowl or jug, mix the egg yolks, sugar and cornflour. Pour the hot milk onto the egg mixture, stirring all the time. Pour back into the pan and cook gently over a low heat, stirring constantly until the custard thickens and just starts to bubble. Turn off the heat and stir in the vanilla.

❊ Carefully run a blunt knife around the edge of each pudding and turn out onto plates or bowls and remove the paper lining. Serve straight away with the hot custard.

Children often find classic crème brûlée too rich, so these little vanilla-flavoured custard desserts are made with semi-skimmed milk instead of cream. Serve with some fresh fruit, such as raspberries, or chopped tinned peaches or apricots.

Creamy caramel custard pots

MAKES 4

For the custard

450 ml (1¾ cups) semi-skimmed milk

½ vanilla pod, split

2 eggs

1 egg yolk

25 g (2 Tbsp) caster (superfine) sugar

½ tsp cornflour (cornstarch)

10 g (½ Tbsp) softened unsalted butter or polyunsaturated margarine, for greasing

For the caramel topping

4 Tbsp light brown sugar

❉ To make the custard, put the milk and vanilla pod in a heavy-based saucepan and gently heat until almost boiling. Remove from the heat, cover and leave to infuse for 10 minutes. Lightly grease four 120-ml (½-cup) ramekin dishes, then place in a small roasting tin.

❉ Preheat the oven to 160° C/325 °F/gas 3. Put the eggs, egg yolk, sugar and cornflour in a bowl and whisk together until thick and creamy. Bring the milk back to boiling point, remove the vanilla pod, then pour the hot milk over the egg mixture, whisking all the time. Strain the mixture into a jug, then divide between the prepared ramekins. Pour enough hot water into the roasting tin to come just over half-way up the sides of the ramekins. Bake for 30–35 minutes, or until lightly set. Take care not to overcook – the custards should still be a little wobbly when you take them out of the oven. Carefully remove the ramekins from the hot water and leave them to cool on a wire rack. Once cold, chill in the refrigerator for at least 2 hours.

❉ Scatter the light brown sugar evenly over the top of the chilled custards and grill under a preheated hot grill for 2–3 minutes, or until the sugar has melted. Leave to stand for at least 5 minutes before serving.

v n

These cupcakes are a great way to encourage children to eat more vegetables without them even noticing! A drizzle of lemon frosting adds a finishing flourish to each cupcake, but if you prefer, dust the cakes with a little icing sugar, instead.

Frosted carrot cupcakes

MAKES 12

For the cake mix

100 g (½ cup) caster (superfine) sugar

150 ml (⅔ cup) sunflower oil

1 tsp finely grated unwaxed orange zest

2 eggs, lightly beaten

100 ml (scant ½ cup) orange juice

3 medium-sized carrots, about 250 g (9 oz), peeled and finely grated

75 g (¾ cup) walnuts or pecans, roughly chopped

175 g (1½ cups) self-raising flour

1 tsp ground cinnamon

For the frosting

100 g (1 cup) icing (confectioners') sugar

1½ Tbsp lemon juice

Zested strips of orange and/or lemon rind, to decorate (optional)

❋ Preheat the oven to 180 °C/350 °F/gas 4. Place twelve paper cake cases in a bun tray.

❋ Put the sugar, oil and orange zest in a mixing bowl and beat together for a few seconds until combined. Beat in the eggs a little at a time. Stir in the orange juice, carrots and nuts. Sift the flour and cinnamon over the mixture, then fold in using a large metal spoon.

❋ Divide the mixture evenly between the cake cases. Bake the cupcakes for 15 minutes, or until well-risen, golden-brown and firm to the touch. Allow the cakes to cool in the tray for 5 minutes, then transfer to a wire rack.

❋ To make the frosting, sift the icing sugar into a bowl and mix in enough lemon juice to make a thick, smooth icing. When the cakes are cool, drizzle a little icing over the top of each cake and scatter with some citrus zest, if liked, and leave to set. Store the cakes in an airtight container and eat within 3 days of making.

Variation: *Instead of carrots, courgettes (zucchini), or a combination of both, can be used for these cupcakes.*
Nutritional note: *Carrots are a super source of beta-carotene, a powerful infection-fighting and immune-boosting anti-oxidant. Cooking releases carotenes, so you get at least double the amount of carotene from cooked carrots than raw ones.*

With its crunchy oat and seed crumble topping and yoghurt-moistened sponge, this nutritious bake is ideal for packed lunches or for an after-school snack. The slices may also be served warm with custard as a dessert.

Apricot slices

MAKES 8 SLICES

For the topping

50 g (½ cup) plain (all-purpose) flour

2 Tbsp rolled oats

2 Tbsp sunflower seeds

2 Tbsp light brown sugar

40 g (3 Tbsp) polyunsaturated margarine, melted

For the sponge

100 g (1 cup) self-raising flour

Pinch of baking powder

½ tsp ground cinnamon

50 g (3 Tbsp) light brown sugar

50 g (⅓ cup) ready-to-eat dried apricots, finely chopped

1 egg, lightly beaten

25 g (2 Tbsp) polyunsaturated margarine, melted

100 ml (scant ½ cup) Greek yoghurt

175 g (½ cup) apricot jam (jelly)

❋ Preheat the oven to 180 °C/350 °F/gas 4. Grease and line the base of an 18-cm (7-in) deep square tin. To make the topping, mix all the dry ingredients together in a bowl. Drizzle over the melted margarine and stir with a fork. Set aside.

❋ For the sponge, sift the flour, baking powder and cinnamon into a mixing bowl. Stir in the sugar and apricots. Blend the egg, melted margarine and yoghurt together in a jug and mix into the dry ingredients. Turn the mixture into the prepared tin and gently level the surface. Drop spoonfuls of the jam all over the top of the sponge, then spread out as evenly as possible, almost to the edge of the tin. Scatter the topping over the top of the jam. Bake for 30 minutes, or until the topping is lightly browned and a skewer inserted into the middle of the cake comes out clean. Leave to cool in the tin, then carefully remove and cut into eight slices. Store in an airtight container for up to three days, or wrap each square in clingfilm or foil and freeze for up to a month.

Tip: *If the jam is stiff, soften it first, by beating for a few seconds in a bowl. Avoid spreading the jam right to the edges of the tin as it may stick and burn.*

Even children who refuse to try rice pudding will love this banana version. The dried bananas soften as they cook, flavouring and sweetening this dessert.

Banana rice pudding

SERVES 4

15 g (1 Tbsp) polyunsaturated margarine

50 g (2 oz) dried bananas, broken into small pieces

50 g (¼ cup) pudding rice

750 ml (3 cups) semi-skimmed milk

A little freshly grated nutmeg (optional)

✳ Preheat the oven to 150 °C/300 °F/gas 2. Use the margarine to grease a 900-ml (4-cup) ovenproof dish. Put the banana pieces and pudding rice in the dish.

✳ Pour the milk into a small saucepan and gently heat until it reaches boiling point (or heat in a jug in the microwave). Pour the hot milk over the bananas and rice, then stir to mix. Sprinkle a little grated nutmeg over the top, if liked. Bake for 1¾–2 hours, or until the rice is cooked and most of the milk has been absorbed, stirring once halfway through cooking. Allow to cool for a few minutes before serving.

Tips: *If cooking in individual dishes, add an extra 75 ml (⅓ cup) milk and cook for 1½–1¾ hours.*
✳ *This dessert may also be served cold. Leave it to cool, then stir in 150 ml (⅔ cup) fromage frais. Spoon into individual serving dishes and top with a small spoonful of fromage frais, sprinkled with a little grated chocolate.*
Nutritional note: *The slow cooking of this pudding concentrates all the goodness of milk, supplying a good amount of protein and many vitamins and minerals – in particular calcium, vital for bone development and growth.*

These moist little cookies have a soft texture and are quick and easy to make. Apple sauce has been used to replace some of the fat and gives them a delicious flavour as well.

Smart cookies

MAKES 16

50 g (¼ cup) polyunsaturated margarine

125 g (½ cup) caster (superfine) sugar

1 egg yolk

125 ml (½ cup) unsweetened apple sauce

175 g (1½ cups) plain (all-purpose) flour

½ tsp bicarbonate of soda (baking soda)

75 g (¾ cup) porridge (rolled) oats

✳ Preheat the oven to 190 °C/375 °F/gas 5. Line two baking sheets with baking parchment. In a bowl, beat together the margarine and sugar until blended, then beat in the egg yolk and apple sauce. Sift the flour and bicarbonate of soda over the mixture and stir in with the rolled oats to make a soft dough.

✳ With lightly floured hands, roll the mixture into walnut-sized balls and place on the baking sheets, spacing slightly apart. Use the palm of your hand to flatten the cookies a little. Bake for 15 minutes, until firm. Allow to cool on the baking sheets for a few minutes, then transfer to a wire rack. When completely cold, store the cookies for up to a week in an airtight container.

Variation: *For raisin and peanut cookies, stir 40 g (¼ cup) each of raisins and chopped unsalted peanuts into the mixture before adding the flour and oats.*
Nutritional note: *Oats are an excellent source of soluble fibre, which can help reduce high blood cholesterol levels (so these cookies can be enjoyed by adults as well as children). It also helps to slow the absorption of carbohydrate into the bloodstream, resulting in a more gentle rise and fall of blood sugar levels and helping to control 'mood swings'.*

This tasty dessert with its caramelised apple topping and pastry-like base is similar to the French Tarte Tatin, but is less rich and much lower in fat. It's especially good served with home-made vanilla custard (see page 143).

Topsy-turvey apple tart

SERVES 4

125 g (1 cup) plain (all-purpose) or wholemeal flour

1 tsp ground cinnamon

50 g (¼ cup) light brown sugar

25 g (2 Tbsp) butter, cut into cubes

25 g (2 Tbsp) reduced-fat cream cheese

1½–2 Tbsp cold water

4 large dessert apples, about 500 g (1 lb 2 oz) in total

1 Tbsp orange or lemon juice

✷ Sift the flour and cinnamon into a mixing bowl, stir in 1 tablespoon of the sugar, then rub in the butter and cream cheese until the mixture resembles breadcrumbs. Sprinkle over the water (you will need the larger amount if you are using wholemeal flour) and mix to a soft dough. Wrap in clingfilm and chill in the refrigerator for 30 minutes.

✷ Preheat the oven to 200 °C/400 °F/gas 6. Lightly grease a round 23-cm (9-in) fixed-based shallow cake tin and line the base with baking parchment. Peel and thickly slice the apples. Put the remaining sugar and orange or lemon juice in a non-stick frying pan and heat gently, stirring occasionally until the sugar has dissolved. Add the apple slices and cook for 6–8 minutes, until they are starting to soften. Transfer the apples and juices to the prepared tin.

✷ Roll out the pastry on a lightly floured surface to a circle the same size as the tin, then place on top of the apples. Make a few holes through the pastry with a skewer, to allow steam to escape, then bake for 20 minutes, or until the pastry is lightly browned. Leave in the tin for 5 minutes, then carefully turn out onto a serving plate. Remove the lining paper, cut into quarters and serve straight away.

Tip: *If the fruit gives out a lot of juice during the initial cooking, lift out the apple slices with a slotted spoon, then boil the liquid until syrupy.*
Nutritional note: *Apples contain immune-boosting antioxidants and are high in soluble fibre, which is important for a healthy digestive system.*

Great for lunchboxes and as an after school-snack, these satisfying cookies are packed full of healthy ingredients to restore flagging energy levels.

Muesli cookies

MAKES 16

125 g (½ cup) polyunsaturated margarine

5 Tbsp demerara sugar

1 egg, lightly beaten

125 g (1½ cups) high-fruit, sugar-free muesli

50 g (½ cup) wholemeal flour

1 tsp baking powder

½ tsp ground cinnamon

❋ Preheat the oven to 190 °C/375 °F/gas 5. Put the margarine and sugar in a mixing bowl and beat together until light. Gradually add the egg, beating well after each addition. Stir in the muesli, then sift over the flour, baking powder and cinnamon, adding the bran left in the sieve.

❋ Roll the mixture into walnut-sized balls, then place on two baking sheets lined with baking parchment, spacing well apart to allow room to spread. Flatten the cookies slightly with the palm of your hand.

❋ Bake for about 15 minutes, or until dark golden. Allow to cool on the sheets for 5 minutes, then transfer to a cooling rack and leave until completely cold. Store in an airtight container for up to a week.

Tip: *Choose a muesli that contains your child's favourite dried fruits and nuts; the tropical fruit versions are particularly delicious in these cookies.*
Nutritional note: *Dried fruit is a concentrated source of many nutrients. Up to 95 per cent of the energy they contain comes from natural sugars and their fibre content ensures that the glucose obtained from the sugars is released slowly into the blood stream.*

Many children who aren't big on fruit will enjoy lightly cooked fruit, topped with a crunchy topping. Here, fresh apricots are used, but when not in season, drained tinned ones make a good alternative, or use fresh sliced eating apples or pears.

Crunchy oat fruit crumble

SERVES 4

675 g (1 lb 8 oz) fresh nectarines, stoned and sliced, or apricots, stoned and chopped

1–2 Tbsp caster (superfine) sugar

50 g (½ cup) plain (all-purpose) or wholemeal flour

50 g (½ cup) porridge (rolled) oats

50 g (¼ cup) light brown sugar

50 g (¼ cup) polyunsaturated margarine

50 g (½ cup) skinned hazelnuts, roughly chopped

✳ Preheat the oven to 190 °C/375 °F/gas 5. Put the fruit in a 1.3-litre (6-cup) ovenproof dish and sprinkle with the caster sugar (the amount used depends on the sweetness of the fruit and personal taste).

✳ Put the flour, oats and light brown sugar in a mixing bowl, then rub in the margarine. Stir in the hazelnuts. Sprinkle the crumble mixture over the fruit and bake for about 25 minutes, or until the fruit is soft and the topping golden brown and crisp. Allow to cool for a few minutes before serving with custard, yoghurt or ice cream.

Tip: *To make it easier to rub in the margarine, freeze it first, then work it into the mixture as quickly as possible, using your fingertips. Butter may be used if you prefer.*

Nutritional note: *Fresh nectarines and apricots, like many orange-coloured fruit and vegetables, are a useful source of beta-carotene, an important antioxidant which protects the immune system.*

Children love jelly (jello); it makes a simple light dessert and is great for party fare. This orange version is made from fruit juice and contains fresh orange segments and grapes to boost your child's fruit intake.

Fresh orange wobble

SERVES 4

600 ml (2½ cups) freshly squeezed or pure orange juice

4 tsp powdered gelatine

2 medium oranges

125 g (½ cup) seedless white or black grapes

✳ Spoon 4 tablespoons of the fruit juice into a small bowl. Sprinkle the gelatine over and leave to soak for 5 minutes. Place the bowl over a pan of near-boiling water, leave for 2–3 minutes, then stir until the gelatine has dissolved. Cool for 5 minutes, then stir the dissolved gelatine into the remaining orange juice in a jug.

✳ Peel the oranges with a sharp knife, removing all the white pith, then cut into segments between the membranes (do this over the jug to catch the extra juice). Divide the orange segments between four individual serving dishes. Share out the grapes as well, then pour over the jelly (don't worry if the grapes float to the top). Chill in the refrigerator for at least 3 hours, or until set.

Tip: *Very small children can choke on large whole grapes, so chop them into smaller pieces if necessary.*
Nutritional note: *A single orange provides more than twice the recommended daily intake of vitamin C, which promotes healing and helps with the absorption of iron in the diet. This water-soluble vitamin cannot be stored by the body, so it is essential to give your child a selection of fruit and vegetables on a daily basis.*

Index